*Daring to
Be Different*

Project Sponsor

Western Historical Manuscript Collection,
University of Missouri–Columbia

Special Thanks

Claudia Powell, Western Historical Manuscript Collection
Chris Montgomery, State Historical Society of Missouri

Missouri Heritage Readers
General Editor, Rebecca B. Schroeder

Each Missouri Heritage Reader explores a particular aspect of the state's rich cultural heritage. Focusing on people, places, historical events, and the details of daily life, these books illustrate the ways in which people from all parts of the world contributed to the development of the state and the region. The books incorporate documentary and oral history, folklore, and informal literature in a way that makes these resources accessible to all Missourians.

Intended primarily for adult new readers, these books will also be invaluable to readers of all ages interested in the cultural and social history of Missouri.

Other Books in the Series

Arrow Rock: The Story of a Missouri Village, by Authorene Wilson Phillips

Blind Boone: Missouri's Ragtime Pioneer, by Jack A. Batterson

Called to Courage: Four Women in Missouri History, by Margot Ford McMillen and Heather Roberson

Catfish, Fiddles, Mules, and More: Missouri's State Symbols, by John C. Fisher

Five Stars: Missouri's Most Famous Generals, by James F. Muench

Food in Missouri: A Cultural Stew, by Madeline Matson

George Caleb Bingham: Missouri's Famed Painter and Forgotten Politician, by Paul C. Nagel

German Settlement in Missouri: New Land, Old Ways, by Robyn Burnett and Ken Luebbering

Hoecakes, Hambone, and All That Jazz: African American Traditions in Missouri, by Rose M. Nolen

Immigrant Women in the Settlement of Missouri, by Robyn Burnett and Ken Luebbering

The Indomitable Mary Easton Sibley: Pioneer of Women's Education in Missouri, by Kristie C. Wolferman

Into the Spotlight: Four Missouri Women, by Margot Ford McMillen and Heather Roberson

The Ioway in Missouri, by Greg Olson

Jane Froman: Missouri's First Lady of Song, by Ilene Stone

Daring to Be Different

Missouri's Remarkable Owen Sisters

Doris Land Mueller

University of Missouri Press
Columbia and London

Copyright © 2010 by
The Curators of the University of Missouri
University of Missouri Press, Columbia, Missouri 65201
Printed and bound in the United States of America
5 4 3 2 1   14 13 12 11 10

Library of Congress Cataloging-in-Publication Data

Mueller, Doris Land, 1927–
 Daring to be different : Missouri's remarkable Owen sisters / Doris Land
Mueller.
   p. cm. — (Missouri heritage readers)
 Includes bibliographical references and index.
 ISBN 978-0-8262-1897-1 (pbk. : alk. paper)
 1. Owen, Mary Alicia, 1850-1935. 2. Owen, Luella Agnes, 1852-1932. 3. Owen,
Juliette A. 4. Owen family. 5. Saint Joseph (Mo.)—Biography. 6. Sisters—
Missouri—Saint Joseph—Biography. 7. Women—Missouri—Saint Joseph—
Biography. 8. Women intellectuals—Missouri—Saint Joseph—Biography.
9. Women pioneers—Missouri—Saint Joseph—Biography. 10. Saint Joseph
(Mo.)—History. I. Title.
 F474.S18M84 2010
 977.8'132030922—dc22
 [B]
                                                              2010017120

⊚™ This paper meets the requirements of the
American National Standard for Permanence of Paper
for Printed Library Materials, Z39.48, 1984.

Design and composition: Kristie Lee
Printing and binding: Thomson-Shore, Inc.
Typefaces: Palatino and Bellevue

To Rebecca Schroeder—

Indefatigable editor, gentle mentor;
Tireless worker, and cherished friend

Contents

Acknowledgments

I am grateful for the assistance of so many people in the writing of this book: for information that Jean Eberle, author of *The Incredible Owen Girls,* shared with me; for materials provided by staff members Linda Endersby and Kate Keil of the Missouri State Museum and by Clyde Weeks, executive director of the St. Joseph Historical Society and Robidoux Row Museum; for the generous service rendered by staff members of the St. Joseph Public Library, Main Branch, the St. Louis Public Library, and the Missouri Western University Library; to Robert Wallace Orr for snippets of Owen family lore; and for the ongoing suggestions offered by Jody, Kate, and Maggie of my critique group. And, finally, I greatly appreciate the ongoing support given by my husband, who was always ready to stop what he was doing to proofread or critique another chapter, or to take over one of my duties to give me more time to write. Thank you!

Daring to
Be Different

1

An Introduction

For a female child born in the mid-1800s in St. Joseph, Missouri, or for that matter anywhere in the United States, opportunities available to her as she grew up would have been severely limited by her sex. The struggle for woman's rights in the United States had just begun, and a long and difficult battle lay ahead for women who sought the right to own property, get an education, or work in fields long reserved for men. The right of women to vote or receive equal pay for equal work lay many years in the future. This was the period in which the Owen sisters were born and grew up.

From about the middle of the nineteenth century, women's vague longing for greater freedom became more specifically focused on issues such as access to professional and legal equality. The year 1848 is often cited as the beginning of the movement for woman's rights. At Seneca Falls, New York, three hundred women and men gathered and developed a document called the "Declaration of Rights and Sentiments," which was based on concepts established in the Declaration of Independence. It included a plea to end discrimination against women in all spheres of society. Sixty-eight women and thirty-two men signed the historic document, which included the first formal demand for women's right to vote.

Opposition to woman's suffrage became fierce. It included the liquor interests (mostly working underground), political machines, the Catholic hierarchy and other religious leaders, and business interests. Many industrialists feared that women would use the right to vote to improve the conditions of working women. Not until 1890 did the first state—Wyoming—grant women the right to vote in all elections. In April 1919, Missouri governor Frederick D. Gardner signed a law to allow Missouri women to vote in the presidential election, and on August 26, 1920, the Nineteenth Amendment to the United States Constitution was ratified by Congress, giving all women the right to vote. Only one signer of the 1848 Seneca Falls resolution lived to see women get the vote. Charlotte Woodward Pierce had been a teenager when she drove a horse-drawn wagon from her home in Waterloo, New York, to attend the historic gathering. In her lifetime she witnessed a revolution in the role of women in American society.

In the 1800s, a woman's role was largely restricted to the private sphere, where she was expected to personify the virtues of piety, purity, submissiveness, and domesticity. The primary expectation for a girl child was marriage, usually while still in her teens, followed by the birth of a baby every two or three years until her childbearing years were over. If she came from a well-to-do family, she would be a better "catch" and have a better opportunity to marry because any property or money she had or inherited would automatically come under the control of her husband. She could not sign a contract, make a will, or sue in a court of law. Her husband could arbitrarily apprentice her children or assign them to a guardian of his choice. Any effort by married women to retain any legal identity or independence had little chance of succeeding.

Middle-class women of the nineteenth century could share the economic and social status of the men but were excluded from the economic opportunities that maintained that status. The glorification of the go-getter businessman and the intrepid pioneer coexisted with an increasing restriction of middle-class women to domestic and ornamental functions. Elizabeth Cady Stanton, one of the early leaders in the woman's rights movement, detailed the legal disadvantages of married women in an address to the New York legislature. A wife had "no civil existence, no social freedom. . . . She can own nothing, sell nothing. She has no right even to the wages she earns; her person, her time, her services are the property of another. . . . She can get no redress for wrongs in her own name."

Should a woman be unable or unwilling to become a wife, few alternatives were open to her. If she had acquired an education, she might look forward to teaching in elementary grades—but usually not in higher grades, which would be taught by a male teacher, however poorly qualified, if any were available. As a teacher, she would continue to live with and care for her aging parents or perhaps board in the homes of her students, in some cases moving from home to home during the year. If she was not prepared to teach, her outlook was still more bleak. Skill with a needle and thread might offer her the opportunity to sew for the more affluent ladies of the community, at least as long as her eyesight held out. Or, possibly, she could operate a boarding house. If all else failed, she could hope to live with a relative, who might expect her to serve as an unpaid maid of all work. Career opportunities open to women were few indeed and certainly did not include becoming a physician, a lawyer, a business executive, or even a stenographer or a bank teller. When considering employment for women, most men did not think of educated middle-class women who might want to pursue a career but only of those from poor families who had to work to survive. Michael Katz, in "The Origins of Public Education: a Reassessment," published in the 1876 winter issue of *Education Quarterly*, concluded that there were four occupational alternatives for women: domestic service, dressmaking, work in a mill, and prostitution.

But some exceptions occurred, and after the Civil War women gradually were able to move into the public arena, especially as writers or artists. In their book *Hardship and Hope: Missouri Women Writing about Their Lives, 1820–1920*, editors Carla Waal and Barbara Oliver Korner identify several well-known women writers, among them Kate Chopin and Laura Ingalls Wilder. Sculptor Vinnie Ream, who attended school in St. Joseph during the 1850s, was the first woman, as well as the youngest person, to receive a federal art commission for her official statue of Abraham Lincoln. During the same period, three sisters in St. Joseph dared to be different in spite of the limited opportunities available to them in the late nineteenth and early twentieth centuries. In so doing, they transcended their time.

Mary Alicia, born in 1850, Luella Agnes, born in 1852, and Juliette Amelia Owen, born in 1859, were the daughters of James Alfred and Agnes Jeanette Cargill Owen. James Owen was an ambitious and successful lawyer, real estate broker, and writer on business and financial matters. His wife, though having made the conventional marriage at eighteen, was by all accounts a strong-minded woman, better educated and more forward looking than most of her peers. Mary, Luella, and Juliette all became leading authorities in fields at that time reserved for men while also maintaining the social relationships expected of them and demonstrating great modesty about their accomplishments.

Each of these unique women was fascinated by a different aspect of Missouri's history and each devoted much of her life to its study. Mary, the eldest, became a folklorist and ethnologist who wrote books, articles, short stories, songs, and poetry; collected stories from the African American community in St. Joseph; and visited Indian reservations in nearby states to observe and record traditions that had survived the forced migration west of Native American tribes. Luella, known to family and friends as Ella, became a geologist and as a member of that male-dominated profession earned the respect and admiration of her colleagues in the field. Juliette, the youngest member of the family, in addition to gaining respect as an ornithologist, an expert on birds, was also a watercolor artist, translator, and writer.

The Owen sisters had the advantage of having been born into a family of some wealth. They were physically well provided for and their parents could afford to see that they received the best education available to girls at the time. The three succeeded because each of them seemed determined to live up to her potential despite the social pressures and gender prejudice of the time. Although expected to marry well, they remained single. Even their parents, though supportive in many ways, sought to impose restrictions on their activities, insisting that they write under pen names so the Owen name would not appear in print. Her parents denied Luella the experience of the cave explorations she longed to undertake until after her father's death.

Although their sister Florence, and brother Herbert married and had families, Mary, Ella, and Juliette all chose to remain single, and each distinguished herself in a career not usually followed by women. While quietly fulfilling the roles expected of maiden women in the social life of St. Joseph, they also made outstanding contributions to the professions of their choice.

This is their story.

2

Saint Joseph
The Place and Its People

The lives and career choices of Mary, Luella, and Juliette Owen were deeply influenced by their hometown of St. Joseph, Missouri. Mary, the oldest of the three, was fascinated from childhood by the stories and songs she heard from members of St. Joseph's African American community and her discoveries at the nearby Indian burial ground. The burial ground was described by family friend J. B. Moss as "a wonderful place to find wild fruits, such as crab apples, choke cherries, mulberries, black and red haws, hickory nuts. . . . On these hunts for fruits and nuts were often found many Indian arrowheads, beads, stone pipes and war clubs." It was the Indian artifacts that interested Mary and led to her later study of American Indian arts and traditions.

Luella, the second sister, also drew inspiration from St. Joseph, but she was fascinated by the geography and geology of her environment: the unique soil known as loess and familiarly dubbed "sugar dust"; the hills, which were rapidly being smoothed out as the city grew; the unique characteristics of the Missouri River with its surrounding rocks and bluffs; and the awe-inspiring beauty of underground caves all intrigued her.

Like her two older sisters, Juliette, the youngest of the Owen children, was keenly interested in St. Joseph and the environment in which she grew up. From the time she was a very young child, she loved the world of nature—the prairie grass, wild flowers, nuts, birds—everything in the natural world. Jean Fahey Eberle, author of *The Incredible Owen Girls*, quotes Juliette as saying, "From my earliest childhood I have had a passionate love for birds and flowers. I remember looking with wondering delight on the velvety upturned faces of the variously tinted pansies that bordered the paths."

If any one of the three, Mary, Luella, or Juliette, could have stepped back in time fifty or one hundred years, she might not have recognized the site of St. Joseph as it had been in its early days. Even as late as 1840, ten years before Mary's birth in 1850, St. Joseph was still only a village made up of a huddle of cabins on the Missouri River.

The spot on which St. Joseph stands was sometimes described as "a cup in the hills along the great Missouri River." According to legend, it was once a gathering place for American Indians, and various Indian tribes came to the site to settle differences and forge alliances. Some tribes considered these "everlasting hills" to be consecrated ground. They believed it had once been the home of their gods; ailing tribal leaders came from far and near to die there. Mary heard stories of the earlier days, when native tribes believed the rays from the beautiful sunsets at this sacred place formed an invisible bridge they called Wah-wah-ha-nawah over which the souls of the departed crossed on a direct route to Paradise. It was, as Indians would tell her later, "the holiest place on earth." In her book, *The Sacred Council Hills*, Mary describes the imposing ceremonies she imagined had taken place on the spot where St. Joseph's courthouse later stood:

It must have been a thrilling spectacle and beautiful as well, when the . . . warriors, sentinels of the morning star, the day bringer, stood . . . softly tapping the sacred drum as the hurrying dawn brightened the eastern sky, their strokes growing strong as the lights increased till, with fury of

sound—booming drum and shouts of exaltation—they
called the tribe to a frenzy of song and concerted movement,
then pious quieting to the sun appearing above the eastern
horizon. Equally beautiful and thrilling but indescribably
mournful, was the farewell to the sun at day's decline, and
to the soul following the shining track to find its way to
Paradise.

In the view of most European settlers, however, the early period of St. Joseph's history was primarily the story of French-
Canadian fur trader Joseph Robidoux III. Born in St. Louis on
August 10, 1783, to Joseph and Catherine Robidoux, he was in-
troduced to the fur trade at an early age by his father. As early
as the 1790s he had traveled up and down the Missouri River
on trapping expeditions. Robidoux married Eugenie Deslisle in
St. Louis in 1800 but was widowed soon after his son Joseph IV
was born. After his wife's death, he returned to the trading post
the French called "La Post du Serpent Noir," later known as the
Blacksnake Hills Post, established in 1803 on the future site of
St. Joseph.

In 1805 a daughter, Mary, was born to him and his Indian
wife there. He later became widely known for his numerous
"country marriages" to Indian women and the half-Indian children he fathered. When his father died in 1809, he took over
the responsibility for the family business, and in 1814 he married Angelique Vandry of St. Louis, with whom he had eight
children. When Missouri became a state in 1821, St. Joseph and
the area known as the Platte Region remained Indian territory
and several Native American tribes had villages and hunting
rights in the area, including the Ioway and the Sac and Fox. The
Robidoux clan, younger brothers and sons of Joseph Robidoux
III, were very successful in competing with other St. Louis trading companies. Tanis C. Thorne wrote that in 1828 the French
Company of St. Louis paid Joseph Robidoux "to stay out of the
Indian Country," and in the early 1830s he bought the rights to
the Blacksnake Hills Post, which later was sometimes known as
Robidoux's Landing.

Joseph Robidoux III was closely associated with the history of St. Joseph until his death in 1868. Born in St. Louis in 1783, only two decades after the founding of the trading post there, he became a successful fur trader and settled at the Blacksnake Hills Trading Post in the early 1800s. He officially founded St. Joseph in 1843. (Courtesy of the State Historical Society of Missouri)

A description of Joseph Robidoux, quoted in Sheridan Logan's book *Old Saint Jo*, depicts him as "dressed in an old, red flannel shirt, his trousers strapped around his waist, on his head a slouched hat, and so tanned and weather-beaten that it was difficult to tell whether he was a white man, a mulatto, or an Indian." At the mouth of Blackwater Creek, now the site of Jules and Second Street, Robidoux built a nine-room house of hewn logs, surrounding it with a stockade; it soon became the largest trading post in the region. Settlers and Indians alike came long distances to trade at the mills and store—but it must have been a wild and lonely place in which to live. Large gray wolves were numerous in the area and their howls were so loud and incessant that at times sleep was impossible. Moreover, the wolves were not only midnight prowlers but were often seen in the daytime, alone and in packs.

During the 1820s and 1830s, life became increasingly more difficult for the Native Americans living in the Platte region. As eastern tribes that were being pushed west moved into the area, increasing numbers of impatient American settlers encroached on tribal hunting grounds in what was still Indian territory. The game upon which the Native Americans depended for both food and furs to trade was disappearing. Travelers wrote of the poverty in which the Ioway were forced to live, and Indian agents warned that some tribes could not survive without more help from the government. The Ioway leader, White Cloud, had tried to adapt to the "White Road" as American officials hoped all Native Americans would do. He settled at Agency, near St. Joseph, and farmed as his American neighbors did. Greg Olson, in his book *The Ioway in Missouri*, quotes a speech White Cloud gave to William Clark and others at a council near Prairie du Chien in 1830: White Cloud proudly reported, "I have succeeded pretty well in following your advice . . . I have learned to plough and now I eat my own bread and it makes me large and strong . . . I follow your advice in everything . . . Even my children are at work making cloth."

Following the "White Road" led to White Cloud's death at the hand of a young man of his own tribe four years later. The

White Cloud, a leader of the Ioway Indians, reported that as a young man he had led many war parties against the Osages. He later became spokesman for his tribe, and one American admirer said of him, "White Cloud is the greatest orator I ever spoke to." At a treaty council in Washington in 1824, White Cloud declared that although the "French had no right to the country in the forks of the Mississippi and Missouri they sold to the Americans," he agreed to relinquish it. He settled near St. Joseph with his family in the late 1820s to try to follow the "White Road." (Thomas McKenney and James Hall, *History of the Indian Tribes of North America, 1836–1844,* courtesy of the State Historical Society of Missouri)

This portrait of Francis White Cloud, White Cloud's son and successor, was painted in the winter of 1836–1837 in Washington. (Thomas McKenney and James Hall, *The Indian Tribes of North America,* courtesy of the State Historical Society of Missouri)

incident, Olson wrote, began when a rumor spread that a Sac and Fox raiding party was on the way to rob the Omaha Indians of the annuities they had received at Fort Leavenworth. "The Ioway sent a messenger to warn the Omaha . . . [who] altered their route of return to avoid the supposed Sac and Fox war party. As they made their way up the west side of the Missouri River, the Omaha stumbled on a small group of Ioway . . . a skirmish ensued in which the Omaha killed the son of the Ioway leader

Crane." Against White Cloud's wishes, a party of young men set out to avenge the death but was not successful. Later, when the U.S. government failed to "deliver justice" in the case, a small war party of twelve Ioway men killed six Omaha men and took a woman and child hostage as punishment for the death of Crane's son. Believing the U.S. government, not the Omaha or the Ioway, should take the lead in settling the matter, White Cloud helped the Indian agent capture the Ioway men he believed were responsible for the death of the Omaha. One of the captives vowed to kill White Cloud and, managing to escape from Fort Leavenworth while awaiting trial, he kept his word. Raising a war party, he tracked down and killed the Ioway leader who had once said he "was almost a white man."

In the early 1830s, Missouri residents and political leaders had begun to petition the U.S. government to remove the Native Americans from the Platte region to make the area available for settlement. In 1837 government negotiators, with the help of Robidoux, completed the "Platte Purchase," in which various Indian tribes gave up their rights to some two million acres—of which the Blacksnake Hills was a part. The Ioway and the Sac and Fox relinquished their claims for the sum of $7,500. An aging William Clark took part in the transactions, one of his last duties as Indian superintendent, and in March 1837 President Martin van Buren declared the area part of the state of Missouri. Soon settlers from the east were streaming into the fertile northwest corner of Missouri.

The Ioway and other Indians mourned the loss of their villages and hunting grounds but, seeing the tide of new settlers, realized they would have to move farther west. Sheridan Logan records a legend that when White Cloud's son, Francis White Cloud, who had married Joseph Robidoux's daughter Mary, realized the white man intended to take the land and remove his people, he sought the guidance of the gods as to whether or not to fight to keep it. He went up to the sacred spring, high on a hill, and saw, growing all around, the plantain weed, known to the Indians as "white man's foot." Everywhere it grew, the white man had come to stay. Understanding this to be the answer to his prayer, White Cloud "covered his face and wept bitterly." When he arose, he went back down the hill to tell his people that "the white man's foot has come to wipe out the trails of the Red man forever," and he led them across the river to their new home in what is now northeast Kansas.

According to Sheridan Logan and others, in 1839, two years after the Platte Purchase had been opened to white settlers, three men came to meet with Robidoux, intending to purchase the site of the Blacksnake Hills post for a previously agreed-upon amount of $1,600 in silver. But somehow during the evening, while the men were playing cards, a misunderstanding arose, and Robidoux refused to close the deal. Historians speculate that he may have deliberately caused the argument because he had changed his mind about selling the post. Perhaps he had already decided to establish the town himself.

The Missouri state legislature formed Buchanan County in 1839, and by 1845 increasing numbers of new settlers had led to the organization of the additional counties of Platte, Andrew, Holt, Atchinson, and Nodaway in the former Platte region. Joseph Robidoux had invited two men, Simon Kemper and Frederick W. Smith, to draw up town plans for him to consider. Kemper offered a plan with wide streets and parks, while Frederick Smith, an emigrant from Prussia who had grown up in Europe and was used to the narrow streets of European cities, proposed a design with narrow streets. Reportedly Robidoux said, "I want to sell my land in lots, not give it away in streets," and finally he chose the plan with narrow streets. Kemper had suggested Robidoux for the town's name, but Smith recommended naming it St. Joseph, in honor of Robidoux's patron saint, and proposed that streets be named for various members of Robidoux's family.

Robidoux filed his plan with the clerk of Common Pleas in St. Louis on July 26, 1843, the official founding date of the fledgling city. As the settlement grew, Robidoux continued to be one of St. Joseph's leading citizens in civic and financial matters although visiting missionaries and others told stories of polygamy among his family members and gambling and excessive drinking at his establishment. In his later years, a rumor spread that Robidoux

This sculpture of Francis White Cloud by Claudia J. H. Packer commemorates the Platte Purchase of 1837. Commissioned by the City of St. Joseph's Parks, Recreation, and Civic Facilities Department, the statue, funded by a grant from the Bradley Foundation, was dedicated in 2004. The statue is located at Southwest Parkway at Hyde Park Drive in St. Joseph. (Photograph by Christopher Schroeder)

once locked his alcoholic son, Joseph Robidoux IV, in a cellar
to force him to deed over land that he had inherited from his
mother.

Joseph Robidoux III died in 1868. Years later, in writing of him
in *The Sacred Council Hills,* Mary, who had been eighteen years
old when he died, wrote,

> Joseph Robidoux, with his intimate knowledge of life knew
> their [the Indians'] reverence for the place and was, we must
> suppose, familiar with their legends, so he rededicated it,
> this time to his patron saint, Saint Joseph. He was a good
> Catholic, but so liberal in his views that he set apart a build-
> ing site for every religious denomination of which he knew
> the name. For the temple of justice he reserved the favorite
> Council Hill, since known as Court House Hill.

On his journey up the Missouri to Yellowstone, John James
Audubon wrote of the site in his journal in May 1843: "We
reached the Blacksnake Hills settlement, which is a delightful
site for a populous city. The hills are 200 feet above the level of
the river, and slope gently down . . . to the beautiful prairies that
extend over thousands of acres of the richest land imaginable."
Another description of St. Joseph in its early years appeared in
the *St. Joseph Gazette* in August 1845: "[When] I first saw the site
of St. Joseph, then known as Black Snake Hills . . . a spectator (or
a speculator) could not well fail to be attracted by the scenery
. . . near where the town stands, the bluffs, by a graceful curve,
sweep toward the river, and present upon their many gradual
slopes, most attractive slopes for rural dwellings."

Throughout the 1840s, traffic through St. Joseph to the west
steadily grew. One early guide to the Oregon Trail advised that
for emigrants "leaving from Ohio, Indiana, Illinois and Northern
Missouri, Iowa and Michigan . . . St. Joseph is the best point."
In *The Oregon Trail Revisited,* Gregory Franzwa noted that as a
starting point, "the strongest rival to Independence was St. Joseph, and, in fact, from the days of the gold rush on, it eclipsed
Independence in the volume of traffic headed west." After gold

was discovered in California in 1848, gold seekers came to realize that St. Joseph was an ideal departure point they could reach by steamboat. Thousands of Americans, as well as visiting Europeans, headed for the gold fields, and St. Joseph was the place where many purchased their supplies and outfitted their wagons. Almost overnight it became a boomtown in which the chief industries were outfitting travelers and freighting supplies or goods to the west. Logan quotes an observer of the westbound traffic who wrote, "There was one continuous line of wagons from east to west as far as the eye could reach."

By 1850, the year Mary Alicia Owen was born, St. Joseph was one of the busiest spots in the nation, and in 1854 a Swiss immigrant who had settled near the town wrote his brother, "St. Joseph . . . is the largest place between St. Louis and San Francisco and is destined to be the greatest city in western America. It is now the chief terminus for the California, Oregon, and Mormon Trails. The Rocky Mountain trappers and the Indian traders of the plains are supplied from this market." During the 1850s its population doubled. Reportedly the richest men in town at the end of the decade were Joseph Robidoux and John Patee, who built the Patee House hotel in the late 1850s. Described as the "largest and finest hotel west of the Mississippi," the Patee House had 110 guest rooms.

One of the earliest settlers in St. Joseph, James Cargill, was also thriving. In early autumn 1843, he, his wife Agnes Gilmore Crookes Cargill, and their children arrived at the Robidoux Landing. Despite the fact that it was a dreary, cold day and raining heavily, almost the entire community, whites and Indians alike, had rushed to the riverbank at the foot of Francis Street as they usually did when they heard the whistle of a steamboat downriver. Up and down the Missouri River, the arrival of a steamboat was always an exciting event. When Cargill stepped down the gangplank of the luxurious steamboat *Lexington,* he was greeted by the town's founder himself, Joseph Robidoux. But the scene at the riverfront—the noisy crowd of roughly dressed settlers, the Indians, the muddy streets, the mingled odors of animal skins and wet clothing—must have been a daunting one, at least for one of Cargill's daughters, who burst into tears and pleaded to be taken back to Virginia.

The captain of the Lexington invited the Cargills to stay overnight on the boat while Robidoux arranged for one of his French-Indian tenants to vacate part of a log house for the new family's temporary shelter. Within a few days, Cargill had purchased a fertile section of land east of the village and built a shed to protect the mahogany furniture the family had brought with them. Lumber with which to build their permanent home, which the Cargills named Burr Oak Grove, had to be hauled in wagons from Weston, thirty miles away. The move to St. Joseph was James Cargill's third and final move westward. Born April 4, 1789, in Liberty, Maine, of emigrants from Scotland and northern Ireland, he had moved as a young man to Pittsburgh where he prospered in the lumber business. In 1829, his westward yen took him to Wheeling, Virginia (now West Virginia), where he amassed a large fortune outfitting settlers heading for Tennessee and Kentucky. In the early 1840s after the death of a sister and business losses, Cargill decided to move farther west.

Cargill was not disappointed in his move to St. Joseph. He soon made up his earlier losses. Starting with an orchard of fruit trees and ornamental shrubs brought from Virginia, he raised wheat, corn, and hemp, which became his largest crop. Hemp was in demand for making rope and was also woven into coarse cloth. Cargill established a steam-powered flour mill beside the Missouri River, the first one west of St. Louis. Large for its time, it operated three shifts a day. The Cargills had brought two slaves to Missouri, leaving others in Virginia in order not to separate families. Later on, they acquired more slaves, including "Aunt Mary" and "Uncle Adam." Mary was an excellent cook, and Adam was so dexterous that when he "broke" hemp, his day's work was usually double the average output of 100 pounds. Reportedly, Cargill always paid him the wages of an extra hand.

Five years after the family's arrival in St. Joseph, Cargill's eighteen-year-old daughter Agnes married James Alfred Owen, another newcomer to the city. According to family history, James Owen was the great grandson of Baron James Owen, one-time vice chamberlain of North Wales. Owen was born on May 20, 1822, on his father's farm in Henry County, Kentucky. His father, Nelson Reed Owen, died when the boy was ten. At age seventeen, after he had been forced out of his home by his abusive stepfather, he began to study law. When two of his uncles in Missouri, Ignatius and John Owen, wrote urging him to come west, he traveled by steamboat to St. Louis and overland to present-day Platte County where he taught school for a year. In 1847, he settled in St. Joseph and began to read law with Judge Solomon L. Leonard, and in the fall of 1848 he was admitted to the bar.

James Owen and Agnes Cargill were married on August 3, 1848. As he became a member of the affluent Cargill clan, Owen remained determined to make good on his own in his new home. The young couple apparently lived for a time with the Cargills; in the 1850 census, James and Agnes Owen and daughter Mary were counted as members of the Cargill household. Although this was not an unusual housing arrangement for newlyweds at the time, family relations may have been strained. James Cargill, who was brusque by nature, had his doubts about his daughter's penniless husband, and the ambitious young lawyer was keenly sensitive to the contrast between his own situation and the conspicuous prosperity of his wife's family.

Still, Owen and his father-in-law did for a time try to get along, even forming a three-way partnership with Sinclair Miller in the Owen and Miller Steam Flouring Company. Unfortunately the partnership was a dismal failure. Although details are murky, Eberle reports that in 1852 Owen sent James Cargill a terse note that said,

> I understand that a report has been put in circulation to the effect that, at the time I left the mill, I drew a club over you, and that it was only [through] the interference of John Cargill that your life was saved. I wish you to say whether this was so, and whether it was by your authority that such a falsehood has been circulated. An early answer to above will
>   Much oblige
>   James A. Owen

There is no record of an answer to this missive, and to the end of his life six years later, Cargill never again spoke to his son-in-law, although the other members of the two families managed to maintain a somewhat distant relationship. When Cargill died in 1858, his wife continued to live on the family farm with her son George, and the relationship between the families improved.

James Owen went on to become a successful attorney, real estate dealer, and financial writer in his adopted city. He served as city assessor in 1853–1854 and again in 1857–1859. He and his wife became the parents of seven children, five of whom survived: Mary, Luella, Florence, Herbert, and Juliette. And as the Owen family grew, so did St. Joseph.

With the migration of so many eastern families to the new state of California during the 1850s, a demand for faster mail delivery developed. St. Joseph won over Leavenworth as the eastern terminal for the service, partly because the Hannibal to St. Joseph Railroad had just been completed. Planners designed a horseback service between St. Joseph and Sacramento, using young (mostly teenage) men and boys who were excellent riders and good shots—and who were willing to undertake the demanding and sometimes dangerous mission. The Pony Express, as it was called, consisted of a relay of ponies and riders stationed at intervals across the plains. Following a ceremony attended by almost all the leading citizens of the city—including James Owen, as Mary later often told her friends—the first rider left St. Joseph on August 3, 1860, crossing the Missouri River by ferry to begin the historic journey. The service ended in October 1861 after only a year and a half of operation, when an east-west telegraph line was completed, but the Pony Express made St. Joseph one of the best-known cities in the United States. The legendary venture is still remembered and celebrated by the city, and reenactors retrace the 1,966 mile ride from Sacramento to St. Joseph each June.

James and Agnes Cargill Owen had built a new home for their growing family on the corner of Ninth and Jules streets during 1858–1859. It was not an easy time for St. Joseph or the Owen family. Juliette, the youngest of the Owen children, often gave

This sketch shows the first train on the Hannibal–St. Joseph Line as it reached Chillicothe on its way to St. Joseph in 1857. Promoters in St. Joseph called it a "Pioneer Route to the Far West . . . 100 miles farther than any other Railroad." (Courtesy of the State Historical Society of Missouri)

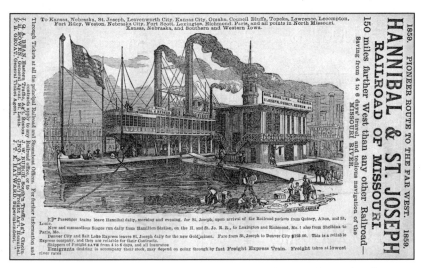

An advertisement for the Hannibal and St. Joseph Railroad had a sketch of the mail packet arriving in St. Joseph from Quincy and Alton, Illinois, and St. Louis to carry the mail farther west. (Courtesy of the State Historical Society of Missouri)

interviews about her family after the death of her parents and older sisters. According to a *News-Press* article of August 22, 1937, the family experienced three terrible summers as the Civil War approached. Agnes Owen often told her family, the paper reported, that the "crop failures, intensive heat, and jangled nerves of that trying time had brought on the Civil War."

The war had a major impact on the Owens and Cargills, as it did on other St. Joseph and Missouri families. The city, like the state, was a house divided. By 1860, St. Joseph had grown from a newly established town to the second largest city in Missouri, although its population of 8,932 lagged far behind St. Louis, which had a population of more than 160,000. Though some of the newcomers to St. Joseph were emigrants from Germany who opposed slavery, the town of St. Joseph and the surrounding area had many Southern sympathizers, some of whom owned slaves. A majority of its pioneer families had come from Tennessee, Kentucky, or Virginia, and many of their descendants, like the Cargill sons, still grew hemp or tobacco using slave labor. James Owen, who also owned slaves, was a strong defender of states' rights, including the right to own slaves, even if it meant seceding from the Union.

Conflict between Southern sympathizers and Union supporters began early in St. Joseph. The impetuous former mayor, M. Jeff Thompson, a native of Harpers Ferry, Virginia, strong supporter of the South, prolific writer of verse, and future "Swamp Fox of the Confederacy," urged Missourians to "Rise in thy might . . . and stand by thy Southern sons in the fight." Trying to calm the situation, town leaders had decided that no flags should be raised in the town by either side, but the newly appointed postmaster wanted to raise a flag over the post office. When consulted, Thompson first said he had no objection. As the flag was raised and crowds gathered around the post office and the German Turner Hall, however, he impulsively climbed to the top of the building, cut down the flag, and threw it into the street. Thompson was soon on his way to try to join the Confederate cause, leaving the city "even more deeply divided," according to historian Robert J. Willoughby, writing in *Robidoux's Town*.

The sympathies of the Owen and Cargill families were with the Confederacy, and the hostile climate created by the war affected the Owen children in numerous ways: broken friendships with children from families who were Union loyalists, the closing of schools as well as many churches, the invasive presence of occupying Union forces, and parental restrictions on their former freedom to roam the nearby hills, prairie, and river bluffs. It was not long until alarming incidents began to occur. First, Agnes Owen's brother John Colby Cargill and his family were arrested in St. Louis on their way to Memphis. In another painful episode, a friend of the Cargills, Captain Reuben Kay of the Jackson Guards, came through Union lines to visit his family and was arrested. When Kay's mother visited him in the old stone jail, she brought him not only tobacco and money but two pistols concealed under her hoop skirt. The jailer later said that since she had "an honest face" he thought he did not have to ask her to take the usual oath that she had no contraband.

As a result, Reuben Kay escaped and fled to Burr Oak Grove in the thin summer clothes in which he had been arrested. The Cargill family gave him food and warm clothing and kept him overnight. The next day, hiding him under a lap robe, they took him on the first leg of his journey back south. When the Union commander learned of Kay's escape, he sent troops to arrest George Cargill, vowing to hang him. The plan was thwarted when the town's Episcopal minister, the Reverend R. W. Weller, rode out to the farm on a bitterly cold January day to warn him. George was able to make a hasty escape, leaving behind his wife and baby, and he lived in the South for the rest of his life. When the Union soldiers found he had escaped, they retaliated by setting fire to Eagle Mills, the Cargill family business. It was totally destroyed and never rebuilt.

The harassment of noncombatants continued. Blue-coated raiders drove off the Cargill livestock and took large amounts of food and clothing. Finally the commander of the Union forces warned Agnes Cargill that he could no longer provide her protection from the looters and advised her to leave the state. Leaving her library with the Owen family and her furniture divided between her daughters, Agnes Cargill and her daughter-in-law and grandson boarded a steamship and began the journey to Wheeling, Virginia, where they joined her son George. They took with them only what they could carry and were allowed to ship only a few possessions, among them the family silver. Unfortunately, the boat carrying the silver sank in the Missouri River.

Historian Preston Filbert, in *The Half Not Told*, paints a bleak picture of life in St. Joseph during the painful days of the Civil War when its divided loyalties and the deprivations and violence it suffered from both Confederate and Union forces and guerilla bands affected everyone. He maintains that of all the young cities of the Midwest, St. Joseph was most affected by the Civil War, noting that residents were "living in an occupied fortress, and left helpless to defend themselves, unable to trust either their government or one another." The notoriety of their former mayor, M. Jeff Thompson, whose actions in Southeast Missouri were widely reported, may well have contributed to the troubles of his neighbors in St. Joseph.

As James Owen watched the harassment of St. Joseph citizens by pro-Union men and saw fatherless families sink into poverty, he seethed with frustration. When Union general Odon Guitar was placed in command of north Missouri, however, he began to enforce controversial reforms to protect civilians, an effort Owen strongly supported. He wrote in his diary that under Guitar, "thieves in the military service were arrested and brought to trial and perpetrators of outrages on the citizens were brought to justice." As a result of Owen's criticisms of the behavior of the Union forces, however, armed troops came to his home on a Sunday evening to arrest him. He was not at home and, as he told it, "a sergeant drove my little daughter Mary to take me from church and confine me in the Guardhouse without charges until morning." He was then released by the commander, but Owen would never forgive the Union, nor would his daughters.

James Owen kept a log during the war, excerpts of which are quoted in *The Incredible Owen Girls* and in *Old Saint Jo*. These entries paint a picture of what life was like for the Owen family during these war-torn years. In late 1861, Owen wrote,

General Odon Guitar, the son of a French emigrant, was
born in Kentucky in 1825 but moved to Boone County
with his parents in 1827. A veteran of the Mexican War,
he owned slaves but above all wanted the Union to be
preserved. In 1862, he formed a regiment of volunteers
known as the Ninth Missouri State Militia, and in 1863
took charge of the District of Northern Missouri, the
counties north of the Missouri River. (Courtesy of the
State Historical Society of Missouri)

> This has been the most eventful year in my recollection. . . .
> Two years ago my property was worth $50,000; today it
> would not bring $15,000 if it could be sold at all. The Revo-
> lution . . . is controlled by maddened factions which daily
> grow more violent. The precipice may be just ahead.

In another entry the same year, he wrote,

> The excitement and apprehensions of the entire year have
> been great. . . . So far, myself and family have escaped out-
> rage or direct injury, with trifling exceptions to both person
> and property. For these we have reason to be thankful while
> nearly all were suffering around us.

The next year, 1862, he wrote,

> My income has been more than my expenses and my family
> are healthy. For these blessings I am thankful. I have been
> greatly annoyed by the Abolition Soldiers. They have fre-
> quently arrested me and I have been ordered to report to the
> Guard House. . . . We have lived in constant apprehension
> of violence.

By 1863, conditions had improved. Owen wrote, "We reside
in our snug cottage at the corner of Ninth and Jules Streets, I
practice Law, rent my property, and trade at my office, . . . Hopes
are fair, though troubles are plenty."

One passionate entry was written after Union general Thomas
Ewing had issued his infamous Order No. 11 of August 25, 1863,
requiring all residents of Missouri's Jackson, Cass, Bates, and
northern Vernon counties who lived more than one mile from
specified military posts to vacate their homes. Approximately
twenty thousand people were affected. "This barbarous order,"
Owen wrote, "drove old men, women, and children out from
their homes in destitution and want, to wander and perish upon
the highways from hunger, cold, and destitution." Order No. 11,
the most drastic action directed against civilians in Missouri by
the Union Army during the Civil War, was initiated in an attempt
to destroy the guerrilla movement by striking at the root of their

Missouri artist George Caleb Bingham, though pro-Union, painted *Martial Law or Order No. 11* to express his outrage over the forced removal ordered by General Thomas Ewing of residents in counties along the Kansas border suspected of supporting the guerrilla forces in the area. When the painting was criticized as propaganda, Bingham admitted he wanted to "keep alive popular indignation." (Courtesy of the State Historical Society of Missouri)

strength, the support of the civilian population. However, a huge outcry from both pro-Confederate and conservative Unionists condemned the order, and Union authorities were forced to retreat from its enforcement.

In addition to war-related issues, the animosity between the Owen and Cargill families flared again. After the death of James Cargill, his widow had assumed the role of farm manager and turned to James Owen as her business adviser, much to the disapproval of her sons. Under her management and with the advice of James and Agnes Owen, she did well despite drought, and she was able to hold onto her land when other landowners had to sell their property. Later when she elected to divide her estate equally among all her children, not favoring the male heirs as was common practice, the sons were indignant. James Owen's

response to their reaction was harsh: he accused the Cargill sons
of selfishly coveting their mother's estate for themselves and of
blaming his wife for encouraging Mrs. Cargill's estate planning
decisions. He ended by noting that "I at length forbade all intercourse between my family and the Cargill family. An experience of 15 years in both social and business intercourse with the
family . . . has brought me to this conclusion."

When the war ended, peacetime brought its own problems
and adjustments. The 1865 Missouri Constitutional Convention,
which freed Missouri's slaves, required citizens to take an oath
of allegiance to the federal government. This so-called ironclad
oath required an individual "to affirm that he was innocent
of any one of eighty-six different acts of supposed disloyalty
against the Union," including not only taking up arms but giving aid or comfort to any hostile person or expressing sympathy
for the South, as a condition for voting or teaching or engaging
in professional life. Few Southern sympathizers could or would
take the oath. This included James Owen, who, only in his early
forties, had to give up his law practice, which must have been a
bitter blow.

One of the consequences of the war and the uneasy early years
of peace, however, was the strengthening of the Owen family
ties. As James and Agnes Owen grew closer to their daughters,
the Owen girls remained primarily under the influence of their
parents. Years before, in 1851, Agnes, her sister and mother, and
three other women had petitioned the first Episcopal bishop of
Missouri, the Right Reverend Stephen Hawks, to send a clergy-
man to St. Joseph. The bishop responded in person and came to
St. Joseph to establish Christ Church. Agnes was the first person
to be confirmed in the new parish, and she and her family were
active in the church and in the community.

The era in which the Owen girls lived was one of continual
change. From its early days, because of its British and Southern
heritage, residents of St. Joseph had aspired to a level of sophistication not usually found on the frontier, holding among other
events an annual celebration of the birthday of Scottish poet
Robert Burns. The residents, proud of their elegant mansions

and social life, declared that St. Joseph was to her citizens what Athens had been to Athenians in the age of Pericles. In just a few years, it had grown from a fur trading post to a frontier town, and during the California gold rush years it had become a boomtown. However, the Civil War divided the city and disrupted the lives of the Owen family, along with the rest of the city's residents.

It took St. Joseph time to recover from a savage war in which it played only a small but a painful part. But, through all the changes, the three Owen sisters chose to spend their lives in the city of their birth. In an article titled "The Road to Paradise," Mary reminisced about some of the changes that had occurred, and closed by saying, "Greater St. Joseph is founded on traditions so old that the memory of men runneth not to the contrary. . . . She has not given up on the Road to Paradise, nor will she; heaven helping her, she hopes to broaden it."

3

The Early Years

"Many women have done excellently, but you surpass them all." This tribute to women, found in the Book of Proverbs, could well apply to all three of the famous Owen sisters. Or perhaps Mary Alicia, who was the eldest and would become the best known of the five surviving children of James and Agnes Cargill Owen, could be singled out as the one who "surpassed them all." All three, Mary, Ella, and Juliette, were conservationists and preservationists by nature, although their interests lay in different areas. All loved the city in which they were born.

Mary worked to preserve the folklore and traditions of St. Joseph's African American residents, whose stories she heard as a child. She studied the art, cultural life, and traditions of those Native Americans on nearby reservations in Kansas and Iowa who had lived, hunted, and traded in northwest Missouri before her birth. Later in her career she wrote of the customs and traditions of the old French founders of St. Joseph, the ways of its early American settlers, and the traditions of new emigrants from European countries moving into the area. Ella, who became a respected scientist, wrote about geological characteristics of northwest Missouri and eventually explored and wrote about the underworld wonder of caves, speaking out vehemently against the destruction she saw. Juliette, in addition to writing articles

View of St. Joseph from the Kansas side in 1861 with the steamboat *St. Louis*. A young Swiss emigrant described some of the steamboats coming upriver to St. Joseph at the time: "Some of the boats had snow-white decks and the softest of Brussels carpeting for the cabins and drawing rooms. . . . The better boats carried pianos and the more pretentious ones carried brass bands which blared as they raced ahead of us. But passengers . . . paid handsomely for it, a single fare from St. Louis to St. Joseph on a speedy packet being thirty dollars, which was as much as father paid for the entire family on our slow boat. Our boat had no band, no pianos." (Courtesy of the State Historical Society of Missouri)

and pamphlets on birds, was an animal lover and advocate, active in the early humane movement. Her drawings of birds and animals for Mary Alicia's collection of African American tales are examples of her affinity for the world of nature.

Unfortunately, no diaries or journals remain to provide a personal record of the Owen sisters' developing interest in the world around them as they grew up in St. Joseph. But their later writings and records available from their early childhood indicate that their "growing-up years" must have been a happy time for them. They lived on a hillside in the shadow of a church, in the comfortable but unimposing gray frame house on the northwest corner of Ninth and Jules streets, which their parents had built just before the war when Mary was about eight years old.

From early childhood, Mary was interested in the lives of members of the African American community and tried to spend as much time with them as possible. She loved to visit the "cabins" and eat roasted nuts, pralines, and other delicacies the "aunties" prepared for her. And she never tired of hearing them tell and retell stories. In the introduction to her book *Old Rabbit, the Voodoo, and Other Sorcerers*, folklorist Charles Godfrey Leland wrote that "she had from infancy an intense desire, aided by a marvelous memory, to collect and remember all that she heard." She herself realized much later that at an early age she had become fascinated by folklore. As she developed an interest in the people around her and their different ways, she wanted to know their histories, their customs, and their ways of worship, and she did not seem to mind asking questions, even after she became older. Her later career was a natural outgrowth of her early fascination with people of different cultures. As Leland noted, her memory was keen, and she was able to retell in detail stories told by the black residents of St. Joseph, Native American women, and others she met. After she became well known for her work in her home state, she confided to a reporter for the *Kansas City Star,*

> I became a folklorist as far back as I can remember—that is, as soon as I could elude relatives and a nurse to visit our curious population. These folks consisted of Canadian French and their part-Indian relatives, Southern people and such of their slaves as remained with them; Yankees who were classified as "black abolitionists," English, Irish, Welsh and Germans, all with their customs unchanged, their prejudices unmodified.

In her book, she described the African American storytellers she met. The first was Aunt Jinny, better known as Granny, who, as Mary wrote years later, "felt herself as important a mistress of the situation there in her cabin, as any queen could in her palace of carved stone." Granny "knew the value of every herb and simple [medicinal plant] to be found in the state . . . was adept in the healing art . . . could 'set' hens so they never lost an egg . . . could tell when to wean a calf or baby and when to plant." Granny, originally from Virginia, described herself as mostly Indian and told of seeing George Washington with her own eyes.

Then there was Aunt Emily, whose "jolly soul was enveloped in billows of fat" and whose "round eyes looked on the world with childhood content." Aunt Mary was "a dark woman of forty, of middle height, well-proportioned and strong." She too said she was "some Injun." Although she had been born in Tennessee, she had spent most of her life in Missouri. She maintained that in both states she "had had some ghostly visitors and serious encounters with his Satanic majesty." Madame Angelique Bougareau, "generally spoken to as 'Mrs. Bougarry,' and spoken of as 'Big Angy,'" said her father was a great French hunter, and her mother was "chile to der big chief of the Iowas." And finally, there was Aunt Mymee, a full-blooded African and daughter of a Guinea "sorceress." According to her accounts of her early life, Aunt Mymee had fled on board a slave ship to escape death at the hands of her countrymen. She claimed to have magical conjuring powers inherited from her mother and delighted in telling people she was a daughter of the Devil.

When the grown-up Mary wrote about the aunties, she described their listener, a blonde, blue-eyed girl child she called "Tow Head," who followed the servants around and listened to their stories. Little Tow Head, who was not always an agreeable child, may have been the fictional persona of the real-life dark-haired, dark-eyed Mary or a composite of other children whose interactions with servants Mary had observed growing up. Tow Head would urge the aunties to tell her stories about blue jays, woodpeckers, rattlesnakes, and rabbits: "Oh, stop fussing, Granny! and tell some stories," she sometimes exclaimed. "Mamma scolds me all I need. You tell me a pretty story." Her accounts of the African American women whose homes she visited to beg for the stories, and the stories themselves, provide a unique insight into the cultural and social life of St. Joseph as well as a sense of the rigid class structure in place that lasted well after slaves were finally emancipated. In St. Joseph, as in other communities in Missouri, life after the war continued very much as it had before, with African Americans who remained still working for their former owners.

The aunties, though sometimes suggesting it was time for her to go back to "The House," entertained Tow Head and cared for her, sometimes shielding her from the natural results of her youthful misadventures. On one occasion, when her curiosity resulted in a fall into "the water buckets," she waited in Granny's feather bed for her clothes to dry while the aunties told stories. On this occasion she insisted on telling a story herself, one that Big Angy had told her, she explained, "that day you took me to her house, and we had such a good time." Granny reminded her Mrs. Bougarry had told her the story to comfort her after the dog bit her because she got too close to the puppies. She agreed, describing how Angy had comforted her. "Angy tied up my leg in a big handful of brown sugar and put a beautiful piece of red calico outside of that, and she let me have the prettiest pup in my lap when we went into the house." Angy had also whistled a tune for her on her eagle bone whistle and had given her "two hands full of prawleens" and told her to eat them all. Then, she recalled, "when I was through crying, she told me the story of the wasp being changed into an oriole." Tow Head told the story as she remembered it:

> When the big black witch from Thunderland came sweeping over field and hollow to fight the witch of the bright Corn Country, the world rang with the sound of her terrible voice and the trees bowed themselves to the ground in terror. In her anger she danced, she whirled, she whistled. She smote the trees, she trampled the prarie [sic] flowers, she scattered the corn-in-the-ear. . . . She fought the witch of the Corn Country, striking her fiercely. She would have prevailed and destroyed the witch and her country utterly had not a wasp . . . stung her in the eye, so that her tears fell and she became calm and weak. . . . Then it was that the witch of the Corn Country was able to chase her back to her own land. Now the witch of the Corn Country was not forgetful, not ungrateful.

Juliette Owen's drawing shows "Tow Head" enjoying the company of Granny and other St. Joseph storytellers. It appeared in *Old Rabbit, the Voodoo, and Other Sorcerers,* published in London in 1893. (Courtesy of the State Historical Society of Missouri)

She took . . . the wasp and besought him to ask for whatever he desired, promising . . . that it should be granted him. Immediately he answered that he and his wife wished not to be wasps, whom everyone hated, but birds, well beloved by all. At once, the wasps had their wish and became orioles; but, because some wasp nature was left, they did not build their nests as other birds do, but made gray pockets to hold their eggs, which from afar looked like wasps' nests; and as they did, so do their children do to this day.

Once when Granny sent Tow Head home, promising her a story later, the "auntie" who took care of the house and had been looking for her everywhere caught her at the door to clean her up because the new minister was in the parlor and wished to see all the children. She was overcome "with a certain chill of bashfulness in her soul" and "had barely strength to sidle up to the dignified minister's knee and tell, when asked, her name, her age, the length of time she had attended Sunday School, and her impression that there were twelve commandments and seven to ten apostles. Growing bolder, she stated to that worthy man that she could sing."

When the minister asked what hymns she could sing, she named "Little grains of water, little drops of sand," and "Lord dismiss us." But, she added, "cabin songs were a great deal nicer than hymns."

Puzzled, the minister asked,

"What are cabin songs, my dear child?"
To the dismay and everlasting shame of her parents and grandparents, and to the speechless amazement of that good ecclesiastic from "Down East," Tow Head piped . . .
"Jay-buhd a-settin' on a hickory lim',
"He looked at me, I winked at him,
"I up wid a rock an' I hit im on de shin,
"An' dat's de way I sucked 'im in."

As a result of the minister's visit, "Tow Head did not make her appearance in the cabin, as she expected, the evening after her interview with the minister, nor for many evenings there-after." The grownups in the family "were suddenly awakened to the necessity of making her acquainted with the writings of Matthew, Mark, Luke, and John. . . . Jay Bird and Woodpecker were for the time being forgotten . . . but one night mamma had a headache and grandma a visitor, so away went Tow Head to the cabins again."

She had been gone so long Granny pretended not to know her, but Aunt Mary told her the story of the Woodpecker and the Blue Jay she begged for.

When the Owen children reached school age, it was a foregone conclusion that they would attend private schools. There were as yet no public schools in St. Joseph, still a frontier town. The few private schools that did exist were held in the homes of well-bred ladies or gentlemen who needed income or simply wanted to provide educational opportunities for children. They usually did not accept students younger than seven, and preference was given to those children who could already read and write. The girls' mother, Agnes Owen, who reportedly taught school be-fore she was married, probably the slave children at Burr Oak Grove, taught Mary to read and write at home, as she would later do with her other children. When Mary reached the age of seven, she attended Miss Bell's private school, where later Ella, two years younger than she, would join her. It was expected that Florence, Herbert, and, eventually, Juliette would follow. How-ever, these opportunities for schooling were not to last, for by the time Mary was ten years old, the threat of war was intensifying. When the Civil War began, Mary and Ella were taught at home again for several more years. Most schools closed during the Civil War and did not reopen immediately at the end of the war. All teachers were required to take the "ironclad oath," and those who had supported the South were ineligible. Nevertheless, St. Joseph did manage to attract teachers, and during her late teens, Mary began taking classes at Patee College. Formerly a luxuri-ous four-story hotel opened by John Patee in 1858, it had proved larger and more luxurious than practical for its time and place. The historic building went on to serve twice as a girls' school.

In addition to taking classes, Mary also began accepting invitations to give dramatic readings and recitations for various church and civic groups. After the Civil War, women's groups began to sprout up all over the country, and lectures, readings, and recitations became very popular events. Mary was seemingly beginning to consider what she wanted to do with her life. The Civil War had hastened the emancipation of women. The shortage of men nationwide after the war led to a greater need for workers and resulted in more accessibility to jobs for women who needed to work. M. L. Rayne, in her book *What Can a Woman Do; or, Her Position in the Business and Literary World*, included endeavors for educated middle-class women such as the writing of book reviews, art criticism, and children's columns as well as giving readings—of poems and prose—to the short list of appropriate occupations. She declared that "there was nothing derogatory to the dignity of any lady in giving . . . readings or recitations."

In 1868 Mary went East to attend the newly opened Vassar College, near Poughkeepsie, New York. The founder, Matthew Vassar, was interested in the education of girls and women, and the school had opened in 1865 as Vassar Female College. Whether the decision to attend Vassar was Mary's idea or a family decision is not known. In any event, it must have taken a great deal of courage for her to leave her family and her frontier home town for the rarified intellectual atmosphere of Vassar College, a school attended in large part by students from abolitionist families with very different backgrounds and different perceptions of slavery, politics, and the woman's rights movement, among other issues.

Mary attended Vassar for only a year, and it is not known why she did not return. Her father recognized his daughter's intelligence and was willing to provide her with the best education opportunities available. Mary must have been encouraged that no longer were matrimony or school teaching the only life choices open to her. She could not help being influenced by the changing social climate in which progressive women were striving to achieve new rights for members of their sex. By the time

This watercolor portrait of Mary Alicia Owen, painted by her sister Luella, provides a rare glimpse of her during her early years in St. Joseph. A second cousin, John P. Cargill of Kansas City, gave it to the St. Joseph Museum in the 1950s along with a self-portrait by Luella and a portrait of Juliette. The paintings are not dated, but staff at the St. Joseph Museum believe they were created around 1880. (Courtesy of the St. Joseph Museum, Inc.)

she returned to St. Joseph after her year at Vassar, and after taking stock of her own strengths and interests, Mary was ready to make a career choice—she would become a writer. Since Ella was still in high school, and Juliette in elementary school, their career decisions were yet to come.

As Ella, the second sister, born in 1852, was growing up, her interest first focused on the shells and fossils that turned up when the road in front of the Owen house was graded. She wondered why there were seashells outside her front door in St. Joseph, Missouri, when the nearest sea was more than a thousand miles away. She also noticed that when one of the road crew made a vertical cut in the soil, it did not crumble like ordinary dirt but remained as firm as a wall. Years later, her curiosity would stand her in good stead when she wrote about loess—the finely ground soil that once covered the region around St. Joseph like a blanket. Her reports would make her the leading expert on this rare geological formation—and when she wrote articles about it she would be able to cite the exact street locations for her findings. Loess is a light-brown rock powder left behind after glaciers from the Ice Age ground south. This dust is so fine it easily becomes airborne. From Sioux City, Iowa, south to St. Joseph, Missouri, are found some of the deepest loess hills in North America—up to two hundred feet deep of highly compacted windblown dust.

With her scientific mind, Ella was intensely curious about everything in the world of nature. She was active and adventurous and delighted in exploring the creeks, river bluffs, and caves near the Missouri River. Who knows what inspired Ella's early interest in caves? Although the St. Joseph area has no caves of note today, in earlier times small caverns may have existed in limestone outpourings along the Missouri River bluffs. As J. Harlen Bretz wrote in *A Comprehensive Description of Missouri Caves,* "No one will ever know how many caves Missouri has." The youthful Ella and her friends would have explored any caves they discovered. Ella's Kentucky and Virginia relatives may have been another source of information, as caves are plentiful in both states.

Ella's natural bent for physical sciences was supported to some extent by her parents, although they tried to discourage her interest in rocks and caves, pressing her to concentrate instead on the more ladylike subjects of astronomy or chemistry. The *Who's Who in St. Joseph* reports that Ella was privately ed-

This 1855 drawing shows the bluffs above St. Joseph, a part of the distinctive landscape of the area that inspired Luella Owen to a lifetime of research about the natural world. (Courtesy of the State Historical Society of Missouri)

ucated. Certainly her mother was her first teacher; during the Civil War when the schools were closed, she again studied at home. Following the war, when the new public coeducational high school opened at Tenth and Edmond streets, Ella became a student there while Mary continued her studies at home. Like Mary, Ella listened closely and remembered what she heard, and she graduated as the class valedictorian. Although for many young women of the time, high school graduation marked the end of their schooling, Ella no doubt planned to continue her own education, again with assistance and encouragement from her parents—especially her mother, who was reportedly very ambitious for her daughters. Moreover, the woman's rights movement was beginning to create a national climate in which "a good marriage" would no longer be the only choice open to women.

Even before Ella completed secondary school, two events occurred that strongly influenced her choice of scientific specializations. First, in 1869, the remains of eight mastodons were uncovered near Sedalia, Missouri, and this event brought geologists and archeologists from all over the country to examine and report on the findings. It is possible Ella visited the site and became more certain of her career choice. Mastodon remains had been discovered in Missouri before. As Ernst A. Stadler wrote, in 1838 Albert C. Koch, an emigrant from Germany who had a museum of oddities in St. Louis, heard of remains found in Benton County and "rushed out to disinter the bones of an animal as large as an elephant." The next year he dug up more prehistoric bones south of St. Louis. The mastodon remains Koch managed to dig up in Benton County in 1840 became known as the "Missouri Leviathan." He first displayed the Leviathan, which he had reconstructed inaccurately, in his museum in St. Louis and invited Missourians "to come and see the gigantic race that once inhabited the space you now occupy." Later he took the Missouri Leviathan on a tour of the United States and Europe, eventually selling it to the British Museum, which paid for a new and more accurate reconstruction of the mastodon. Although Koch's discoveries occurred before Ella was born, the new finds would have brought back memories of the Missouri Leviathan.

The next important event in Ella's education occurred closer to home when a group of St. Joseph businessmen arranged to have a bridge built across the Missouri River. Ella watched the progress of the bridge building and from time to time talked with the construction workers. When the bridge was completed in 1873, Horace Carter Hovey, a Presbyterian minister from Kansas City—who was also an ardent spelunker, or cave explorer—came to St. Joseph to view the bridge and to explore nearby caves. His arrival gave Ella and her friends many opportunities for properly chaperoned explorations. She and Hovey became friends as well as fellow cave explorers. He confided to her his plans to write books about American caves for the general reading public, and his enthusiasm for this project started Ella dreaming of one day writing a book of her own about Missouri caves. Hovey went on to become the author of numerous books about celebrated American caves including Kentucky's Mammoth Cave and other caves east of the Mississippi River. Ella must have been familiar with his book *Celebrated American Caverns*, which begins,

> The crust of the earth is pierced by natural cavities that exist like the hills above them, in an endless diversity of sizes, shapes, and structural peculiarities. Just as there are prairies and table-lands without a semblance of a hill, so there are broad areas of non-cavernous rocks. Only a limited portion of the globe is favorable to the formation of caves.

One fragment of Hovey's description of cave explorations must have intrigued the intrepid Ella: "Steadying myself for a moment . . . I reach with the right foot for the first little notch, barely big enough for the toe of my boot . . . I cling to naked rock with one hand, the other holding the torch, and cautiously lower myself to the next notch. Step by step the narrow shelf is gained."

It is little wonder that Ella was strongly influenced by such adventures as Hovey described. In his book on Mammoth Cave of Kentucky, he stipulates that the book is meant "for the leisurely perusal of the general reader," as Ella's later book on the caves of the Ozarks and Black Hills of South Dakota would also be.

Ella was popular with the young men of her community. In addition to being attractive and well brought up, she was an heir of James Owen as well as the granddaughter of James Cargill, and therefore "a good catch." According to Eberle, the Owen descendants whom she interviewed believed that the three Owen sisters did not marry because their mother would take to her sickbed whenever one of them showed an interest in a suitor. But Ella, who was known to be as "brusque and brainy" as her father, had a mind of her own, and she was much more interested in pursuing a career than in snaring a husband. Perhaps the deciding factor was that she would have far fewer freedoms and live a more restricted life as a married woman than the one she enjoyed being single. Although she did not officially join the suffragist movement, she was probably well informed by their thinking. Certainly she was a more "liberated" young woman than most of her peers.

Juliette, the youngest and considered by family and friends the prettiest of this unusual trio of sisters, was born November

Luella Owen as she saw herself in the self-portrait she painted.
(Courtesy of the St. Joseph Museum, Inc.)

3, 1859. She was probably the most indulged of the children, especially after her infant brother, born in 1861—the last Owen baby—died. Like her siblings, Juliette began her education at home. After the Civil War had ended and St. Joseph schools reopened, her parents sent her, along with Florence and Herbert, to private schools to be with children of similar backgrounds. Juliette was apparently a more docile, less adventuresome child than either Mary or Ella. She was closer in age to her sister Florence, born in 1855, and her brother Herbert, born in 1857, than to the two older girls. Although she enjoyed playing quietly with dolls, she also delighted in playing hide-and-seek in the tall prairie grasses or searching for wildflowers and berries with her friends. She loved the outdoors all her life. As Eberle observed, "Most of us briefly notice a fine day or a particularly stormy day. For Juliette Owen, nature always stood in the foreground." Her interest in the environment, which began in childhood, stayed with her for life. She was keenly interested in natural history, birds, and wildlife. Once, when a plague of grasshoppers covered the fields, devastating the trees and the farmers' crops, young Juliette set about to inform herself concerning the plague's effect on local wildlife. Her special love was ornithology, the study of birds, and she became a great admirer of John James Audubon and began to collect his works. She wrote on botany and about Missouri birds, and she excelled in watercolors, which enabled her to paint the birds she loved. Always an animal lover, in later life she became an unofficial veterinarian, and the family home often served as a shelter for injured and abandoned animals.

By the time the three sisters had reached adulthood, each had a clear vision of her goals in life and was dedicated to the attainment of those goals. Mary's formal education had ended with her year's study at Vassar. Ella did not enroll in college but read extensively in her chosen field of geology. Although early twentieth-century biographies of the three Owen sisters report that Juliette attended Vassar, as Mary did, later researchers found no evidence at Vassar that she did; but she was for a time a student at the Patee Female Seminary in St. Joseph. Each sister diligently pursued her special interests outside formal schooling, and Juliette continued her professional growth through participating in conferences and reading in her field.

In the decades following the Civil War, life had gradually returned to normal for the Owen family and other citizens of St. Joseph. James Owen, who with his wife had managed his money wisely during those lean war years, was now able to benefit from the postwar boom and add to his wealth. But, unlike a number of affluent friends and relatives, he did not move away from the business district of the city but continued to live

Juliette Owen, the youngest of the Owen sisters, reportedly when she was about eighteen. (Courtesy of the St. Joseph Museum, Inc.)

with his family in their frame house on Jules Street. As part of their education, James Owen wanted his daughters to be able to conduct their own financial affairs, so he made sure they learned how to manage money and keep accurate records. Their mother, Agnes Owen, keenly aware that married women could not legally control their own money but were subject to their husbands' decisions, could no doubt point out to her daughters examples in the community in which the husband had squandered the family's resources. Although she was not a woman's rights advocate in the traditional sense, she seemingly shared many suffragist views. Eberle believed, "Agnes had felt the first winds of woman's suffrage." *Who's Who of St. Joseph* describes her as possessing "an eager mind and a retentive memory which gave her a solid base for the reading that throughout her long life kept her well informed . . . while still young she became the highly appreciated and valued consultant of her husband." She was not only better educated than most women of her time, but she was fully aware of and actively involved in the family's financial affairs in a full partnership with her husband. She was also active in community and church activities although these seem to have been curtailed somewhat following the early death of the last Owen child, James Arthur, who was born in 1861.

In 1876, when James Owen ran unsuccessfully for lieutenant governor on the Greenback ticket with J. P. Alexander, the Greenback candidate for governor, his wife and his daughters campaigned for him. They of course were not eligible to vote for him, a situation that grieved them, but they could go forth into the community dressed in the shirtwaists and long skirts or day dresses in fashion at the time to encourage their male friends and relatives to cast their votes for him. They could enthusiastically affirm the qualities attributed to him by a local biographer: "As a man, no one dared to assail his sterling qualities, for he possessed remarkable probity, decision, method, energy, and self-reliance. And he was intensely practical."

The last decade of the nineteenth century brought more changes to St. Joseph and to the Owen family. In 1881 Florence Owen married William Bard Orr, and the couple moved to Pennsylvania. The following year, after James Owen had set his son up in the real estate business, Herbert Owen married Hattie Kearney, and the couple made their home in St. Joseph. In January 1890 James Owen became ill, and by early spring he was no longer able to leave the house. The three sisters still living at home alternated between working on their individual projects and caring for their father. He died at home on May 3, 1890. The courts of St. Joseph closed for the day of his funeral.

After James Owen's death, his real estate was divided into six equal shares, one for each of his five surviving children and a one-sixth share for Agnes, instead of the usual one-third share awarded to widows. Although not the conventional estate division, this arrangement was consistent with the Owen family's long-established values. As Owen had arranged, each of the children gave Agnes Owen power of attorney to retain and manage the estate, dividing only the income while keeping the property intact. According to Eberle, records show the first distribution gave each child approximately $22,000, which at the time was a small fortune.

Upon her husband's death, Agnes Owen assumed the role of invalid and reportedly never again left her home on Jules Street. With her son Herbert representing the family in business matters, however, she very capably controlled the family's finances for the next two decades. Whether she was genuinely ill or, as some descendants have suspected, pled illness as a strategy to keep her three remaining daughters at home and unmarried is a matter for speculation. In any event, Mary, Ella, and Juliette made a commitment among themselves after their father's death that two of them would always be at home with their mother, meaning that only one at a time could travel. They kept that promise for more than twenty years, until their mother's death.

During those years the Owen sisters enjoyed the companionship of their family. Florence moved back to St. Louis and spent her winters in Florida, but Herbert's children grew up in St. Joseph, each having a special relationship with one of the aunts. Herbert and Hattie regularly brought their children to visit their grandmother; the children were especially happy if Mary was home—she was after all a "member of an Indian tribe," and she was always interested in every aspect of their lives. When Herbert's daughter Annie Owen made her debut, Agnes Owen paid for the ball, and the three aunts took time away from their careers and caregiving to serve as hostesses at the gala affair. Later, when Annie was married, the three aunts were again there, even though for Mary it meant hurrying back

When James Owen ran for lieutenant governor on the Greenback ticket with J. P. Alexander, who had also come to Missouri from Kentucky, his wife and daughters campaigned for him. As a newspaper in Kirksville predicted, however, there was not "a ghost of a chance for the Greenback ticket." The Democratic candidates swept the state in 1876. (*Portraits and Biographical Record of Buchanan and Clinton Counties, Missouri* [Chicago: Chapman Brothers, 1893], courtesy of the St. Joseph Historical Society and the State Historical Society of Missouri)

early from a meeting in Columbia, Missouri, to attend the wedding. Although Mary, Ella, and Juliette stayed in the family home with their mother, each continued to pursue her career.

Almost two decades earlier, in 1871, when Mary was twenty-one, Ella nineteen, and Juliette only twelve, a woman who was to influence the cultural lives of women in St. Joseph for the next half century moved to town with her husband, the new minister of Christ Episcopal Church. Constance Fountleroy Runcie was the granddaughter of Robert Owen (not related to James Owen), a British socialist who had set out "to reform the whole world," as a reader of his book *A New View of Society* had observed. Robert Owen came to the United States in 1824 and the next year purchased the utopian colony Harmonie, which had been established by German emigrants on the Wabash River in Indiana in 1821. Renaming the community New Harmony, he organized it as a socialist community in an effort to achieve an ideal society. The New Harmony school Owen opened offered concerts, discussions, and lectures for residents as well as schooling for the children. The community dissolved in a few years, but when her father returned to England, his only daughter, Jane Dale Owen, remained in New Harmony and married Robert Henry Fauntleroy, a Virginian.

Constance Fauntleroy was born in 1836. Her father died when she was fourteen, and she and her mother moved to Europe. For five years they lived in Germany, where she became fluent in German and French. They spent time in Italy, and Constance studied with her uncle, Robert Dale Owen, U.S. minister to Naples, but in 1857 they returned to New Harmony. Constance organized and taught a Sunday school class of 125 children, and in 1859 she organized the first women's club in the United States, the Minerva Club. Its motto was "Wisdom is the crowning glory," and the members met every Monday evening to read original poems and stories and debate "timely subjects." Constance married James Runcie in 1861 and moved with him to St. Joseph. In her article "Constance Runcie and the Runcie Club of St. Joseph," published in *The Other Missouri History*, Janice Brandon-Falcone described the impact the remarkable Constance Runcie had on the cultural lives of the women of "the bustling city of twenty thousand souls nestled on the hills that overlooked the Missouri River at the edge of the state." While her sister-in-law, Anne, who had moved with the Runcies, took care of the house and children, Constance continued to write music, welcome the new opera house and other cultural developments in St. Joseph, and "pay little attention to the bandits" prominent in the area, though she did note in passing the rewards offered for Frank and Jesse James.

In 1889, James Runcie died, and his wife and family had to move from the rectory. Constance Runcie wanted to stay in St. Joseph, and she had a plan for a way to support herself from the new home she wanted to build. As Janice Brandon-Falcone wrote, "For a woman of Runcie's social standing, work outside the family home was nearly out of the question." Using the small estate her husband left, the sale of a farm in Indiana she inherited, and a collection the church took up for her, she built a house on the corner of Seventeenth and Jules streets to provide herself with a place of employment as well as a home.

The first floor was one large room with a double fireplace designed for meetings, lectures, concerts, and other events. It served as an excellent meeting place for a women's club, which the women of St. Joseph organized and named for her in 1894. Like the Minerva Club she had organized in New Harmony, Indiana, years before, the Runcie Club offered readings of poems and stories, discussions, and other programs planned and assigned by Mrs. Runcie. Florence Owen Orr, who returned to St. Joseph for a time with her two children after her husband's death in 1897, became a member of the club. As Brandon Falcone notes, the women of St. Joseph used their membership in the club "to assert their claims to take part in public activity," and it "became a means of empowerment and leadership training" for women and "enhanced their position in society without questioning existing social relations." The Runcie Club not only provided empowerment and educational opportunities for the women of St. Joseph, but it provided Mary Alicia Owen and other women who wanted to speak a platform and an audience.

4

Mary Alicia Leads the Way

When Mary Alicia Owen returned to St. Joseph from Vassar, she was undoubtedly welcomed home not only by her family but by her many friends and acquaintances who had not had the opportunity to spend time "back East." They were eager to learn about the social activities, customs, and fashions of the young women Mary had met during her year in New York. For her part, Mary slipped easily back into the social life she had enjoyed before her Vassar year. She continued to write ballads for parlor recitations and to present some of her dramatic readings for church and civic groups.

Behind the scenes, Mary probably enlisted the support of her family in pursuing her newly formed plan to become a writer. She knew that she would have to write under a pen name: at that time no "respectable" woman's name appeared in print except on the occasions of her birth, her marriage, and her death. She also had to decide what to write. After the Civil War, the demand for sentimental fiction had grown rapidly, but she had no interest in writing romantic novels. She decided to try writing for magazines and subscribed to a number of national magazines and new periodicals for women, some of which included a variety of travel articles, political pieces, and short stories. After studying them carefully, she began to send out her handwritten manuscripts to various editors and wait for their responses.

Mary Alicia Owen returned from Vassar to her family home on the corner of Jules and Ninth streets in St. Joseph and soon settled into her new career of writing. In the photograph, she is on the right and Juliette on the left, according to the family member who gave the photograph to the St. Joseph Historical Society. The donor believed the dogs belonged to Mary. (Courtesy of the St. Joseph Historical Society and Robidoux Museum)

She also contacted local newspaper editors, and with her powers of persuasion and charm, suggested that she would be willing to write stories about social events in St. Joseph similar to those carried in eastern newspapers. Adopting the pseudonym of Julia Scott, she wrote about local social events, including visits by celebrities from the East Coast and abroad who toured the western states and Canada in the 1880s. Her column "Julia Scott's Saturday Night" became a popular feature. She wrote book reviews and short stories for the *St. Joseph Gazette* and wrote for and became the literary editor of the *St. Joseph Saturday Democrat*, a short-lived weekly newspaper published from about 1879 to 1883.

Mary was interested in everything about St. Joseph, and she wrote accounts of the city's early settlers and its early history. She enjoyed talking about historic events she remembered from her childhood, and if someone brought up the legendary Pony Express, for example, she could say with authority, "Why everyone always knew the first rider out was Johnny Fry. My father saw him go. Johnny had a little racing mare of his own and won most of the races run along the river bank, but he didn't ride his own horse." Mary had been ten years old at the time the first Pony Express rider left from St. Joseph on April 17, 1860, an event long remembered by the town's residents. The mayor of St. Joseph, M. Jeff Thompson, had presided, and the *St. Joseph Free Democrat* reported, "All [spectators] being desirous of preserving a memento of the flying messenger, the little pony was almost robbed of his tail." Historians have argued about whether it was in fact Johnny Fry or Henry Wallace who was the first rider, but the majority favored Johnny.

Her sister Juliette said of Mary in an interview published in the *Kansas City Star* on January 24, 1941, "I used to tell Mary Alicia that she was a born gossip. She liked to talk about people." She added, "She was interested in humanity in all its manifestations," a trait that must have been helpful to her in gathering notes for her columns. The journalist and poet Eugene Field spent a year in St. Joseph in 1875 and wrote a poem, "The St. Jo Gazette," describing the year when he "hustled around and sweat" to gather news and "helped 'em run the local on the 'St. Jo Gazette.'" He was grateful that "Dr. Runcie let me print his sermons when I had the space."

> The labors of the day began at half-past eight A.M.,
> For the farmers came in early and I had to tackle them;
> And many a noble bit of news I managed to acquire
> By those discreet attentions which all farmer-folk admire,
> With my daily commentary
> On affairs of farm and dairy . . .
> Oh, many a peck of apples and of peaches I did get
> When I helped 'em run the local on the "St. Jo Gazette."

Poet Eugene Field, born in St. Louis in 1850, the year of Mary's birth, worked for the "St. Jo Gazette" for a year, married Julia Comstock of St. Joseph, and returned from time to time to visit his wife's family there. (Courtesy of the State Historical Society)

Unlike Eugene Field, Mary had to gather her news without revealing that she needed it for her column. In an era when poetry was very popular, Mary also published poems and stories in periodicals, including not only *Century Magazine* and *Overland Monthly* but also *Peterson's Magazine* and *Frank Leslie's Illustrated Newspaper.* According to William Clark Kennerly, in his book *Persimmon Hill,* "In this sentimental age, poetry was first aid to lovemaking and was used extensively in courtship . . . any excuse was good for a poem." Mary devoted much of her poetry to descriptions of the natural wonders of her home state, which she had missed in New York, as she demonstrates in "The Homesick Missourian."

I am wearying for my prairies
Where the little rivers run
All fringed with trees and blossoms
That help keep out the sun;
While between lie fields and orchards
And pastures too, galore,
And barns and goodly houses
With children at the door
'Tis my own, my dear Missouri
The land of golden corn,
The sweetest land the wind blows o'er
The land where I was born.
I long to see the clover
Beleaguered by the bees
Far sweeter than the honey
Its fragrance in the breeze.
I want my grassy orchards
Where the big red apples glow
On boughs bent down in garlands—
Eve tried them long ago.
Now they grow but in Missouri
The land of fruit and corn—
The sweetest land the wind blows o'er,
The land where I was born.
I want to watch the hazels
Shake down their winter store,
And the walnuts and the shellbarks
On the earth's leaf-spangled floor.
Life's fullness and life's richness
I can find no other where—
O, my own, my dear Missouri
I am longing to be there
There in my own Missouri
With its hazelnuts and corn;
The sweetest land the wind blows o'er
The land where I was born.

And I want my mighty river
To which its "cricks" all run,
Where the brant are flying over
And the fish leap in the sun;
And my lakes that dimple near it
And the sedge where plovers call
And the lilies where the ducks hide—
Dear Lord, I want them all
That belong to dear Missouri
Land of game and fruit and corn;
The sweetest land the wind blows o'er,
The land where I was born.

In December 1889, Mary's short story, "Taming of Tarias," appeared in *Century Magazine* under the name of Julia Scott. According to Juliette, this was Mary's first published magazine work. Set in St. Louis in 1840, the story was about Tarias, a girl of French and Indian descent, and her tumultuous romance and marriage to a Kentuckian named Dave. Biographers believe this was also the first time Mary published a work in dialect, which later became an integral aspect of much of her writing.

As early as 1876, Mary's own name had appeared in the newspaper about a presentation of "Mrs. Deacon Brown's Story" that she had read to an audience at the local Baptist church, and during the 1870s she became well known in publishing circles as Julia Scott. But the fact that Julia Scott was really Mary Owen was such a well-kept secret that many years later an article cited by Jean Eberle reported, "by 1886 Mary Alicia Owen had definitely decided on writing as a profession." By that time she had been writing stories, articles, and poetry for more than a dozen years, but she kept using a pseudonym until after her father's death and she had established herself as a successful writer.

In addition to her writing, Mary maintained an active civic and social life, attending lectures and other events so that "Julia Scott" could review them for the newspaper. She traveled to resorts and other interesting and fashionable places and submitted travel articles to magazines. In addition, she was a member of Christ Episcopal Church, the Daughters of the American Revolution, the Martina Martin Story Tellers' Club, the Wednesday Club of St. Louis, and the Mary Alicia Owen Story Tellers' Club, a group of society women who told stories and presented dramatic readings in schools and orphanages. No doubt she participated in numerous other social activities and heard many stories of earlier times, which she wrote about decades later in an article published in 1920 in the *Missouri Historical Review.*

Mary also continued to find time to visit her elderly African American "aunties" and listen to their stories, as well as hear the gossip about their friends and their employers. These provided her a unique insight into St. Joseph social life, which was to serve her well in her later work. Her friends in the black community also let her know when voodoo practitioners, who traveled from town to town in the Missouri River Valley, arrived in St. Joseph. Nor did she neglect her childhood hobby of collecting Indian artifacts and trying to find out as much as she could about them. She continued to bring home beadwork, pipes, and other Native American art objects she had "coaxed" tribal members she visited in the 1870s and 1880s to sell to her.

Then in 1888 something happened that would change her life dramatically. A friend, Olivia Proctor, loaned her a book to read. Olivia was the daughter of the English astronomer Richard Anthony Proctor, who did not share the prevailing view that women were frivolous and scatterbrained, and encouraged his daughter and her friends to read and study widely. The book Olivia lent Mary was a collection of folktales edited by the American folklorist Charles Godfrey Leland, who was living in Europe at the time. According to Jean Eberle, "Mary thanked Olivia Proctor for the book and thanked a kind Providence for sending Olivia and her father . . . to St. Joseph." She later said that if her friend had not lent her this book, *Algonquin Legends of New England,* she would have been satisfied to remain a short story writer for magazines for life.

When Mary read Leland's book she saw how similar the Algonquin legends were to the stories that she had heard as a child from St. Joseph's black residents. Years later in a *Kansas City Star* interview she said, "The legends were so like those I had heard in shacks and cabins of my childhood friends." This discovery was to open up a whole new world to her. Mary wrote to Leland, thanking him for the pleasure his book had given her and asking for his autograph. Then, responding to a footnote in which Leland had asked for related items from his readers, she enclosed several of the stories she had written down from her storehouse of childhood memories. This letter was the beginning of a correspondence between them that would last until Leland's death in 1903.

Leland, who was in Italy when he received Mary's first letter, was enthusiastic about the material she had sent. He wrote back immediately asking her to send him more items to use in what he called a "great American dictionary" of "queer words, phrases, rhymes, charms, in short, folklore of all kinds—country people's usages, jokes, etc." He also urged her to write down all the stories she knew and to look for more, advising her to put her tales into a form suitable for publication in a book of her own. As their correspondence continued, Leland became Mary's mentor and her closest friend, and he strongly urged her to pursue her interest in folktales, which she did. Although she continued to write her newspaper column, she no longer had time to write for periodicals once she began the formidable task of preparing her collection of stories for publication.

Some Owen descendants speculate that Mary developed a romantic relationship with Leland, but Jean Eberle disagrees, arguing that "they met rarely, on her trips to Europe . . . surrounded by associates. . . . Besides, his wife or his niece usually accompanied him on their trips." Moreover, when his wife died, Leland continued to live in Italy and Mary continued to make her home in Missouri. But there is no doubt they became close friends. They wrote regularly, and he sent her numerous small gifts. Once she sent him a list of American fancy drinks that he could use in one of his articles.

In 1890, when James Owen died, Mary wrote to Leland, telling him of her father's death. He sent his condolences, and then

Charles Godfrey Leland, Mary Owen's friend and mentor, was living in Florence, Italy, when this portrait was painted shortly before his death in 1903. His biography includes a number of letters to Mary. Born in 1824 in Philadelphia, Leland studied at Princeton University and in Germany at Heidelberg and Munich. The picture is from *Charles Godfrey Leland, a Biography*, by Elizabeth Robins Pennell. (Boston: Houghton Mifflin, 1906, vol. 2, courtesy of the Western Historical Manuscript Collection, Columbia)

wrote again to suggest that she consider participating in the first International Folklore Conference, which was to be held in London in 1891. At first, she hesitated, perhaps reasoning that Leland was simply trying to distract her from grieving for her father. But the idea began to take root; she discussed the possibility with her family, and eventually submitted a paper. It was accepted, and she made plans to travel to England. Eberle reports that she traveled with a friend to the East Coast and joined a group of American folklorists traveling to London for the conference. In

September 1891, she presented a talk on the results of her research at the meeting in London.

Her paper, referred to in the *Times* of London as "Voodoo Magic," was, according to Leland, a sensation at the meeting. In addition to being very well received by the audience, the *Times* published a detailed description of the presentation: "Miss Owen contributed a paper on Voodoo Magic, to the mysteries of which she, alone of white women, has been initiated." The report continued with a detailed account of the steps the ritual required. "Good charms," the paper reported, "were hardest to work, because good is always more difficult to practice than evil." It was helpful if the novitiate possessed a conjuring stone—"a stone black in color, kidney-shaped and very rare." Another requirement was that "After each lesson both pupil and teacher had to get drunk, either by drinking whiskey or by swallowing tobacco smoke."

In 1893, through Leland's influence, the collection of folk tales Mary Alicia had collected in St. Joseph was published simultaneously in England and in the United States under different titles: in London it appeared as *Old Rabbit the Voodoo and Other Sorcerers* and in New York as *Voodoo Tales Told among Negroes of the Southwest.* The stories in the book are in the local dialect Mary captured in her memory during her childhood in St. Joseph, listening to the "aunties" whose homes she visited. Both the text by the author and the stories themselves reflect in detail the beliefs, customs, and practices of the storytellers. Illustrations by Mary's younger sister Juliette and English artist Louis Wain depict some of the animal, bird, and human characters in the stories.

As Mary painstakingly prepared her book for publication, Leland had sent advice about the proper way to present the stories she had collected to the public. In one letter he advised her to keep her writing as natural as possible. "Write your book just as you write to me . . . be as droll as you can." Although he himself had used the Pennsylvania German dialect in his early work in the United States, Leland thought that printing the stories in dialect would make them incomprehensible to many readers. He cautioned her to "remember that your Missouri Negro-English

is difficult for many Americans to understand and almost a foreign tongue for English readers." Above all, he wanted the book
to be readable. Mary did not take this advice too literally; in fact
she rendered the dialect as closely as possible to the way she remembered hearing it.

In Leland's introduction to her book, he explained that these
were not the "pleasing tales for the nursery" made on the "Grimm
principle," which, he wrote, by the time they were printed were
at that stage of development when they were perhaps at their
"prettiest," but also "at their driest." These stories from the United States were "fresh, green and growing leaves," gathered from
residents in Missouri descended from Native American and African American ancestors, in which "the traditions of both races"
were "combined or blended . . . into new life." He noted that
"Mary Alicia Owen . . . had from infancy an intense desire, aided
by a marvelous memory, to collect and remember all that she
learned." In his experience, he wrote, the only other person who
was as thoroughly at home on the subject of folklore as Mary
was a full-blooded Passamaquoddy Indian who had decided to
collect all the "folk-lore . . . of his tribe." Leland wrote of her
book, "As regards novelty and originality of subject, it ranks
among the most important contributions to Folk-Lore." He was
disappointed in her too-exact rendering of dialect and realized
it would be a problem for some readers, but found it especially
interesting that all her material had been gathered from a small
area in and around St. Joseph.

Leland had warned Mary about the possibility that readers
would confuse her folktales with those of Joel Chandler Harris,
published in 1880. *Uncle Remus: His Songs and Stories* was a collection of newspaper columns Harris had written, and in fact the
English publisher may have hoped that readers would remember the popular "Brer Rabbit" when they saw a book about "Old
Rabbit." But despite Leland's concern, Mary went forward with a
form similar to that of Harris. Her "aunties" narrate the stories.

Folklorist William McNeil, in his article, "Mary Alicia Owen,
Collector of Afro-American and Indian Lore in Missouri," published in the 1980 *Missouri Folklore Society Journal*, wrote that the

"success of Harris's Uncle Remus books has tended to obscure the important contributions of other writers. Among the most important of these . . . is a Missouri native, Mary Alicia Owen of St. Joseph." McNeil suggested that although Mary did not intentionally copy the Harris style, she inadvertently helped to disseminate his mistaken idea that "Black Folktales" dealt primarily with talking animals. Even though she collected other types of folktales, Mary, too, chose only animal stories to publish. However, a review of her book in the *Journal of American Folklore* in 1893 pointed out that "the singular feature [of her stories] is at once observed, that instead of being variants of the Negro lore made familiar by Mr. Harris [they] much more closely resemble the Indian tales." McNeil believed that Mary would have had a greater influence in the United States if her friend and mentor Leland had been identified more closely with this country instead of being based in Europe.

In his introduction to Mary's first book, Leland had hinted that she would also be writing a book on voodoo, saying that she had "carefully recorded and will at some time publish her very extensive knowledge of the subject." Mary did begin in earnest to research voodoo, a subject few other scholars had attempted, and she apparently gathered a large body of information relating to voodoo magic. Her information came from many sources—from Leland and other folklorists, librarians, and scholars. She even traveled to Cuba to gather data. She visited the camp of a "gypsy queen" but found that gypsies did not greatly interest her. According to her sister Juliette, "it was old 'King' Alexander who really taught her about voodoo." When Mary met the renowned voodoo doctor, "the king of occult cussedness" as she called him, she recorded many of his beliefs. "Make up your will strong against yourself," he told her, "and you will soon have it strong enough to put down . . . everybody else." Along with his imposing appearance, embellished by a stovepipe hat, and his sudden comings and goings, King Alexander was sometimes a down-to-earth philosopher. "It seems to me," he once told Mary, "conjurin' is mostly whiskyin.'" When he came to town, he would appear mysteriously, always at night. He never stayed

HE CAUGHT HER BY HER LONG, FLOWING HAIR.

The story of the eagle who wanted to become a girl was one of several stories in the "Last Gleaning of the Field" in *Old Rabbit, the Voodoo, and Other Sorcerers*. The drawing reflects the contributions of Native Americans in the St. Joseph area to the stories in Mary Owen's collection. According to Gladys Coggswell, who learned a version of the story from her great-grandfather in New Jersey in the 1950s, he may have heard the story in his youth in Missouri. (Courtesy of the State Historical Society of Missouri)

long in one place, and no one knew where he came from or where he was going. He did, however, take time in his interviews with Mary to teach her a few chants and confide some voodoo secrets to her. She also got from him a smooth black stone from Africa that he called a "jenuinne" voodoo stone, which she later gave to Leland.

When King Alexander and other voodoo practitioners came to town, Mary's friends in the black community helped her arrange to meet with them, and her genuine interest and tact usually was sufficient to encourage them to talk with her. She also knew enough not to bombard them with a list of prepared questions to be answered; rather, she tried to initiate a casual conversation to glean the information she sought, an approach she later advocated for other collectors as well. In a brochure published by the Missouri Folk-Lore Society, she suggested topics to bring up for those interested in collecting Missouri folklore:

> Superstitions connected with great natural objects—tell what you know of the great talking fish in the Missouri River, of the thunder pent up in certain of the Ozark Mountains, of the Indian warrior ghosts that sit around certain sacred springs, etc., . . . beliefs relating to a future—where do the good dead go? What is a ghost carrier? . . . It need not perhaps be said that these are suggestions rather than interrogatories to be fired point-blank at your informant . . . "by indirection find direction out" is often the best method for the folk-lore collector.

When her promised work on voodoo seemed to have hit a snag, Leland wrote, "I am sorry the voodoo business is interrupted, but a strong will, ingenious trickery, and a belief in you will set it right." Mary kept up with her research until, as Eberle put it, "she knew more about the voodoo 'religion' than any [other] white person." But for whatever reason, she vacillated about completing this manuscript and ultimately put it aside altogether. Knowing that voodoo relied on fear and having seen the terror aroused in its victims, she apparently was reluctant to publish the results of her findings. Years later, when her grand-niece confessed an interest in voodoo, Mary told her she had once written a book on the subject that included many of its terrifying symbols and rituals. She added that she had burned the entire manuscript in the fireplace.

However, Mary did use her intimate knowledge of voodoo in some of her articles and stories. In her second book, *The Daughter of Alouette,* voodoo played a central role. This novel, published in London in 1896, told the story of a half-French, half-Indian orphan girl who was reared by a white minister in an American village. In the story, Mary was able to bring colorful characters to life, from the fundamentalist minister to the mixed-race Alouette and the voodoo princess Ahola. The book's portrayal of Ahola was especially compelling—her robes, her throne, her voodoo shrine, even the symbols that decorated her fingernails. *Oracles and Witches* was another fictional work with a frontier flavor that used her research into voodoo beliefs. When she wrote about voodoo, Mary attracted several different audiences: those who enjoyed her ability to mix horror and humor while telling an engaging story; British readers, for whom stories of the American frontier had an exotic appeal; and people who were seriously interested in learning everything they could about witchcraft and the occult.

During the 1890s, Mary traveled to scenic resorts, attended conferences, and visited friends and relatives. When the American Folk-Lore Society was formed in 1888, she became a charter member and later served as its president. In 1893 she went to the Chicago Columbian Exposition, and that year she also gave a paper at the American Folk-Lore Society annual meeting in Memphis, the first of many papers she prepared for the organization. For a long time, she continued to produce her manuscripts in longhand, but eventually she did purchase a typewriter. Later, she found it necessary to employ an assistant who typed her manuscripts from her handwritten material.

She was becoming widely known as an authority on folklore in her home state, as well as in Europe, and she began to focus on statewide collection. In an undated manuscript now on file in the Missouri History Museum in St. Louis, she declared that "no country is as rich in folklore as the United States . . . no state can claim superiority over Missouri in the abundance and variety of this material." She went on to cite numerous examples of customs based on ancient lore. Mary maintained that although many superstitions die out, one class remains—that which relates to ghosts. She closed with the hope that the "treasure of tradition, poetry, and romance" would never be lost.

It was perhaps only natural that after the publication of *Old Rabbit, the Voodoo, and Other Sorcerers,* often referred to as *Voodoo Tales,* Mary's next major project would focus on the lore of Native Americans who had lived in St. Joseph and northwest Missouri. Through regular visits to their villages in Kansas and Iowa, she had maintained her contacts with the Algonquin tribe she called the Musquakie (Mesquakie), known to Europeans as the Fox. During a *Kansas City Star* interview in 1941, Juliette recalled, "There were several Indian Tribes across the [Missouri] river and Sister used to go over and stay with them several days at a time. If she was going to stay all night she sometimes took our brother [Herbert], but more often she went alone. The Tribes welcomed her to their camp because they knew she liked them."

Eventually, Mary reported she had become an "honorary member" of the nearby Mesquakie tribe. When she visited their villages, she was always careful to follow their customs. She did not, for instance, try to speak directly to the men; instead, she spent her time gossiping with the women about the old days. While tradition decreed that women had no say in policy making, Mary observed that Indian women managed to convey their views by carrying out their chores and discussing their opinions within earshot of appropriate tribal elders. Juliette quoted her as saying, "People think the Indians are . . . stoic, but they're not. . . . The women giggle a lot just as we do." Mary continued to make these expeditions to Indian settlements despite the fact that, according to Eberle, when she returned home, she had to take off her clothes, bathe, and put on fresh clothing before her mother permitted her to reenter the Owen home. Evidently Agnes Owen did not trust the quality of the sanitation in the villages.

Since childhood, Mary had collected Native American artifacts she found on the St. Joseph hillsides, and she began asking the tribes she visited about them. In Eberle's words, her growing collection of beadwork, pipes, and household objects made her feel "she was holding the past in her hands." She feared that nineteenth-century progress was transforming the Indians' way of life and that their traditions would soon be forgotten, a belief shared by many anthropologists of her day. The Mesquakie, who had once roamed northwest Missouri, now lived in two locations. Some still lived on federal lands in Brown and Doniphan counties in Kansas, while others now lived in central Iowa, where they had bought property in 1856. Keenly concerned that she might be living at the end of something precious and irretrievable, Mary wanted to preserve the evidence and memories of those earlier times.

Mary once wrote in a letter, "I dare say I was a hundred times among the Musquakie between 1881 and 1898. . . . I had trouble getting my collection. We were always dodging those white idiots the government sent out."

As Alison K. Brown notes in her article, "Beads, Belts and Bands: The Mesquakie Collection," published in the 1996–1997 *Missouri Folklore Society Journal,* Mary's interest in folklore included a wide range of subdisciplines such as local dialects, folktales, and customs. While most of her contemporaries concentrated on reporting statistics or collecting information on "traditional" beliefs, Mary realized that material objects were integral to an understanding of the societies she studied. Although Brown disputes some of her findings, she credits Mary Owen with being "one of the most prominent and knowledgeable non-native authorities on Mesquakie material culture of this period."

In 1897, Mary sent a paper on Mesquakie culture and traditions to be read at the Toronto meeting of the British Folk-Lore Association. She was unable to attend herself because one of her sisters was away from home, and their agreement was that two of the three sisters would always be at home to care for their mother. Mary later agreed to expand the paper into a monograph on the subject. Titled *Folk-Lore of the Musquakie Indians of North America and Catalogue of Musquakie Beadwork and Other Objects in the Collection of the Folk-Lore Society,* it was cited as "a formal anthropological description of the tribe during a clash of cultures." The Folk-Lore Society had the book published in London in 1904. In addition to containing a number of illustrations and a catalogue of the items in her collection, it included folktales and information on Mesquakie origin myth, as well as their history, beliefs, and customs relating to all stages of life—birth and infancy; puberty, courtship and marriage; to death and burial; and to ghosts as she understood them. She also described the various dances she had observed, such as a religious dance and the totem dance.

In his preface to the book, Edwin Sidney Hartland states,

> The introductory paragraph of the Catalogue describes [the value of her monograph and her collection] better than words of mine could do . . . the objects here catalogued are not "merely pretty and picturesque," they are, almost without exceptions, ceremonial. This statement is made for the sake of those students of folk-lore who have warned collectors of wild peoples' property that they should neglect the merely pretty and picturesque, and gather in such objects as are ceremonial.

Mary gave the Folk-Lore Society her extensive collection of beadwork and ceremonial objects, which was exhibited at a joint meeting of the society and the Anthropological Institute in 1901 and then placed in the Museum of Archeology and Ethnology at Cambridge University.

By the early twentieth century, Mary Alicia Owen, then in her fifties, had achieved international stature. She was given a place in the British *Who's Who* even before she was similarly honored in America. She was a life member of both the American and British Associations for the Advancement of Science, as well as of the American Folk-Lore Society. Although she wrote what many consider one of the most important books on black folklore of the nineteenth century, she could often be self-deprecating. On one occasion she responded to a request for a picture from a staff member at the Missouri State Capitol by writing, "I have no photograph. No use perpetuating my kind of looks."

She had first achieved unique access to the almost impenetrable world of voodoo. Then she had embarked on the project to collect artifacts of the Native American tribes who once

This photograph of Mary Alicia Owen appeared in the *British Who's Who* of 1905, more than a decade after her book was published. (Courtesy of the State Historical Society of Missouri)

lived in northwest Missouri, writing a book about the history and customs of the Mesquakie Indians, and describing items in her collection of objects, which she donated to the Folk-Lore Society. Allcorn said of Mary that her books "are most interesting for their eclectic blend of literature and science." Her interests and activities were wide-ranging—from black folklore to Indian artifacts, from ancient history to astronomy, from aviation to genealogy. (Once, with her usual wry humor, she characterized her ancestors as "a hard-headed contrary lot. . . . Some of them at least sarved [served] the Lord as if the devil driv 'em hundreds of years before I was born.")

Charles Godfrey Leland, Mary's longtime friend and mentor, died in March 1903. Ironically, in 1903 Henry M. Belden of the University of Missouri, with whom she was to collaborate for the last two decades of her life, became aware of the survival of traditional folk song and balladry in Missouri. A few years earlier, Harvard professor James Francis Child had published *The British and Scottish Popular Ballads,* a five-volume collection of traditional songs from the British Isles. Child had believed that these songs were no longer widely known and sung. He had tried "to stimulate collection from tradition in Scotland, Canada, and the United States," he reported, but the results had been meager, "as ought perhaps to have been foreseen at this late date."

Belden heard a student sing a song he had seen in the Child collection and found out that many more such songs were known in her community. He was inspired to find out whether such ballads and songs were still widely known in Missouri. He soon found an abundance of evidence that they were and began a half-century-long effort to collect and preserve his adopted state's ballads. Leland, born in 1824 in Pennsylvania, had been twenty-six years Mary's senior. Belden, born in 1865 in Connecticut, was fifteen years her junior. Though Mary never developed the close relationship with Belden that she had with Leland, he had enormous respect for her work. For her part, she became an enthusiastic supporter of the Missouri Folk-Lore Society, established at the University of Missouri in 1906, and was largely responsible for encouraging the broad scope of its efforts. Belden, like many of his contemporaries in England and the United States in the early twentieth century, became primarily interested in the collection and study of songs and ballads. Mary, on the other hand, had set out to study folklore in its many manifestations.

Henry Marvin Belden came to the University of Missouri in
1895. He founded the Missouri Folk-Lore Society in 1906, and
like Mary Alicia Owen set out to collect the oral cultural traditions of Missouri. Belden was primarily interested in collecting
British and American ballads and songs, but the society soon
distributed "Suggestions for Collecting Negro and Indian Folk-
lore in Missouri," reflecting Mary Alicia Owen's interests. With
Owen as president and Belden as secretary, the society soon
gained a loyal statewide membership. (Courtesy of the University of Missouri Archives)

Mary was elected vice president of the Missouri Folk-Lore Society at its organizational meeting in 1906, and in 1908 became president, an office she held for the rest of her life. Her philosophy of folklore can be seen in the society's constitution: "The purpose of this Society is the study of folklore in the widest sense of the term, including the customs, superstitions, signs, legends, language, and literature of all races, especially as they are found in the state of Missouri." Some years later, in writing of "The Significance of Folklore," Mary stated, "Folk sayings—proverbs and the like—are the final distillation of the garnered experiences and observations of humanity." She closed by quoting, "Know then thyself, presume not God to scan, the proper study of mankind is man," and added, "That you may do so, study FOLK-LORE."

Mary Alicia was the first of the Owen sisters to make a name for herself, but she would not be the last.

5

Luella

Geologist, Explorer, Painter, Family Historian

Although she did not become as internationally famous as her sister Mary Alicia, Luella Agnes Owen also gained fame and respect in her chosen field and enjoyed a successful career as a scientist. In 1852, when she was born, St. Joseph was still a frontier town, one of the last U.S. settlements before the beginning of the vast and still largely unsettled American West. There were as yet no paved streets in the city and when it rained, horses hitched to buggies or carriages had trouble making their way through the sticky mud. In her *History of the Growth and Development of St. Joseph*, Nellie Lutz wrote that in the summer of 1853 a steamboat race was held between the *Polar Star* and the *James B. Lucas*. When the *Polar Star* was the first to arrive in St. Joseph, a celebration dinner was set for the next day. Unfortunately, the event had to be held without the women of St. Joseph. The muddy streets made it impossible for them to get there, either by carriage or on foot. As a consolation, the ladies were invited to attend a dance on the deck of the *Polar Star* the next time it docked. The delay, though disappointing, did give them time to buy or make new dresses for the occasion.

Luella was six years old before the Hannibal and St. Joseph Railroad reached her town, and seven and a half when the first Pony Express rider departed. Still, because of the city's rapid growth, as Greg Olson notes, St. Joseph developed an affluent upper class and aspired to a level of sophistication uncommon on the frontier. This seemingly contradictory combination of frontier independence with the impeccable propriety of the time contributed to Luella's ability to fulfill her role as a Victorian lady in St. Joseph society while making a name for herself in her professional life as a geologist, cave explorer, world traveler, portrait painter, and genealogist. Ella, as she was called, chose not to marry, and continued to live at home with her parents and siblings. Eventually, two of her younger siblings married, but even after their parents died, Ella, Mary, and Juliette continued to live together in the frame house on Ninth and Jules, making the Owen home their own.

When asked to provide information about herself, Ella Owen always reported that she was "privately educated." She did finish high school, but no records have been found to indicate that she ever attended a college or female seminary. Even by the 1870s, geology was not a branch of natural science to which women were usually drawn, unlike such pursuits as astronomy, ornithology, or botany. These studies would have been much more acceptable to James and Agnes Owen. In fact, both Ella and Mary, with the full approval of their parents, were protégées of the British astronomer Richard Anthony Proctor, the father of their friend Olivia. A popular writer on astronomy who is best remembered for having produced the first good chart of the planet Mars, Proctor lent Ella many scientific journals for her study, and anecdotal evidence indicates that she read extensively in her field of interest—books, professional journals, and geological maps. She, like her sisters, was a dedicated collector of books, papers, and other paraphernalia related to her interests, and the Owen library must have rivaled the collections of many private and

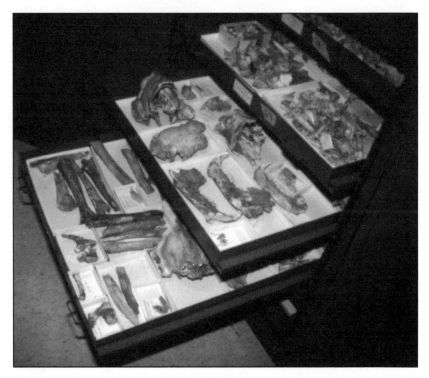

During the early nineteenth century, explorers in Missouri found nu-
merous fossil remains of animals from early geological periods. Albert
C. Koch's energetic promotion of his finds led to a widespread interest
by Missourians and others in the history that lay underground. These
Ice Age bones were found in caves in Missouri and Illinois. (Photo by
Dwight Weaver of bones in the Research and Collection Center of the
Illinois State Museum)

public libraries in Missouri by the time St. Joseph established a
public library in 1891.

By the time Ella graduated from high school about 1870, the
population of St. Joseph had doubled, but not much is known of
her activities from 1870 until her father died in 1890. No doubt
she spent part of her time participating in the social obligations
expected of a young woman from a prominent family, but she
must have devoted a great deal of time to her studies; she may
even have followed her mother's lead, pleading fragile health
to avoid social events that did not interest her and leaving more

time for reading and study. Since Mary is known to have begun
to travel to American Indian villages in nearby states as soon as
the Missouri River bridge was opened in May 1873, Ella may also
have traveled to northern Minnesota to study glacial deposits, to
the Garden of the Gods in Colorado, and to the Grand Canyon in
Arizona, among other well-known sites of geological interest in
the United States. Eberle writes, "Luella left no letters or memoirs in which to trace her itineraries, but from the number of
places she refers to in her writings, she must have logged more
miles than any woman of her time. The whole Missouri River
basin became as familiar to her as the streets of St. Joseph."

The lack of documentation for her life during these years is
due, at least in part, to the fact that she published nothing under her name during this time. At her father's request, she wrote
under a pen name during his lifetime, and her pseudonym has
been lost along with her letters and other personal documents.
Unfortunately for those who would like to know more about
her work, Ella burned much of her correspondence as well as
her field notes and other unpublished papers near the end of her
life.

In one way or another, during the twenty years of her young
adulthood, Ella acquired a broad knowledge of geology and built
a network of influential associates that gave her both the tools
she needed and the respect for her abilities necessary to move
forward in her career as a field scientist. As she continued her
study, she sought to identify a specific area in which she could
make her mark. When she read *A Memoir of an Iron Bridge over
the Missouri River, at St. Joseph, Missouri,* printed by the Detroit
Bridge and Iron Works, with its references to the unusual loess
soil that was so plentiful around St. Joseph, she decided to write
a paper on loess and submit it for publication. She may well have
written first to seek advice from some of the geological experts
whose books and articles she had read. Perhaps it was such correspondence that led her to become acquainted with three men
who became her mentors, her instructors and advisors, and finally, her colleagues. Although Ella was always silent about the
details of her education in geology, she spoke gratefully of these

three men who assisted her with her remarkable achievements. In response to the advice of these mentors she began to investigate geological phenomena in the upper Missouri Valley.

One of her advisers was George Frederick Wright, a nonprofessional geologist and minister. The "nonprofessional" label signified that he did not earn his living in geology but was a private scholar in the field. Ella followed his lead and began to identify herself as a nonprofessional geologist. Wright had graduated from Oberlin College in Ohio in 1859 and in 1860 served for five months as a private in the Seventh Ohio Volunteers; in 1862 he graduated from Oberlin's theological seminary, was ordained, and became pastor of a Congregational church in Vermont. Although he later became a professor of New Testament language and literature at Oberlin, he continued to devote so much attention to geology that he was seldom on campus. Wright's geological interests took him around the globe—to Alaska, Greenland, China, Siberia, and farther—gathering original data for his books, among which were *Man and the Glacial Period* and *Greenland's Ice Field and Life in the North Atlantic*. In addition, he served as editor of the scientific journal *Bibliotheca Sacra* from 1884 to 1920. When he encouraged Ella to attend professional meetings and to submit material to *Bibliotheca Sacra* for publication, she followed his advice.

American geologists in the late nineteenth and early twentieth century spent thousands of hours debating the effects of glaciation, the erosion and scarring of the earth's surface that occurred during the Ice Age. This was a knotty problem to solve because the glacial ice had removed or buried much of the evidence of its movement. The most easily accessible remnants of the Ice Age in northern Missouri are the western border loess hills and glacial erratics, large stones unlike the local rock, which had been transported great distances in the ice, and Ella became interested in studying this evidence of the Ice Age so close at hand.

Ella's second mentor, James E. Todd, grew up in Tabor, Iowa; he also studied at Oberlin College and then at Union Theological Seminary. In 1871, he became a professor of natural sciences at Tabor College. Although he too considered himself to be a nonprofessional geologist, he served in several professional geological positions, including one as state geologist of South Dakota. He wrote a number of articles about his research while at the University of Wisconsin and the University of South Dakota. Ella became familiar with his work, and Todd too became Ella's adviser and then her colleague.

Her third mentor, Newton Horace Winchell, was a professional geologist. Born in New York State, he attended public school in Connecticut and then taught school in Connecticut and Michigan. While teaching in Michigan, he graduated from the University of Michigan and also earned a master of arts degree. In 1871, while at the University of Minnesota, he was recruited to direct the Geological and Natural History Survey of Minnesota. In his twenty-eight years as director, he conducted extensive original research into the state's geology and was responsible for *The Geology of Minnesota*, a six-volume publication prepared with the assistance of his students.

Winchell encouraged Ella to submit her articles to foreign geological journals as well as to domestic publications, and she began to do so. She had started to learn French as a child and continued to study it in high school. After graduation, she worked to gain greater fluency in the language. Her knowledge of French enabled her to write "Cavernes Americaines," the first of several articles she wrote on Missouri caves. She submitted it to *Spelunca*, the bulletin of the French *Société de Spéléologie*. At the time it was published in 1896, she was the only woman member of the society. She also contributed articles to the *American Mining Engineer Journal* and *American Geologist*, among other publications.

Ella's early curiosity about the earth's structure, its rocks, and especially its caves had developed into a consuming passion for cave exploration by her early twenties when she became an ardent member of group cave expeditions led by Horace Hovey. But when Hovey moved from the area, her parents—primarily her father—strongly disapproved of such scandalous behavior as tramping through damp, dark underground caverns. So Ella bided her time while continuing to study the geological journals to learn as much as she could about caves. Frequently she would read of the discovery of new caves, few of which had been explored or scientifically described. She concluded that a perfect project for her would be to explore as many caves as possible and to write of her experiences. This would be a major undertaking, but no effort would be too great if it enabled her to experience the majesty of dazzling underground caves, lighted only by candles or flares, about which she had read.

She didn't actually begin her spelunking—cave exploration— period until about two years after her father died, when she was nearly forty years old. Before she embarked on her cave travels, she planned her campaign carefully, first identifying caves from professional journals and then writing their owners to ask permission to visit them.

Next she put together a sensible explorer's wardrobe consisting of a skirt and boots, a jacket, and an oil-silk hood and cape to protect her head and shoulders from the moisture that dripped from cave ceilings. She even designed a special divided skirt for her explorations—actually a short pair of pants with a pleated skirt that resembled a dress—directing her dressmaker to sew several of these divided skirts. She may even have stitched up the prototype herself on what is considered to be one of the most important inventions of the nineteenth century: the foot treadle sewing machine.

This skirt of Ella's outfit was much shorter than the style at the time dictated—it stopped at knee-high boot tops. "If it is properly made," she declared, "only the wearer need be conscious of the divide." Although she knew that overalls would be even more practical, she stopped short of choosing a costume that would raise too many eyebrows at home. She referred to her outfit as "a costume that is not exactly an artistic creation." Whether she was influenced by the bloomer costume, designed by Elizabeth Miller and made famous by Amanda Bloomer, is uncertain; at least the two concepts were similar, especially after the harem-pant style of the bloomer was modified.

Ella's exploring outfit stood in sharp contrast to the fashions of the day, in which ladies wore skirts so long they picked up dust and mud and tended to trip the wearers on stairs and uneven ter-

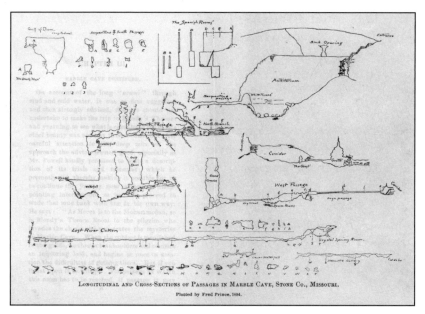

LONGITUDINAL AND CROSS-SECTIONS OF PASSAGES IN MARBLE CAVE, STONE CO., MISSOURI.

Plotted by Fred Prince, 1894.

Fred Prince drew this "only official map" of Marble Cave in 1894, and Luella included it in her book, published in 1898. (*Cave Regions of the Ozarks and Black Hills,* courtesy of the Western Historical Manuscript Collection, Columbia)

rain. By the 1880s and 1890s, the bustle had come into style and the skirts had softened to a relatively slim shape, but there was still no relief from constrictive underwear. Typical undergarments for women included a one-piece chemise and pantalettes that came below the knee and were decorated with tucks and flounces. Underneath all this was the heavy corset, which gave an armor-like rigidity to the silhouette. The styles restricted movement with their multiple layers of clothing, intricate decoration, and sheer abundance of fabric.

Ella wrote to her three mentors to tell them of her proposed cave explorations and to ask for their advice. As she bided her time, she consulted maps and worked out potential travel routes to the caves she planned to explore. On her caving expeditions, she used whatever transportation was available—train, horse and carriage, or mail coach—over barely existing roads and sometimes through trackless forests. Her travel might begin with a train trip to the town or station closest to the cave property. At that point she had to arrange with a hotel, inn, or private home for food and lodging. Then she would find someone to drive her to the cave itself. And, most important of all, she would have to persuade the cave owner to guide her through the cave.

Eberle describes a typical expedition when Ella set out for Marble Cave (now Marvel Cave) in Stone County: "She packed her gear and made an all-day train trip to St. Louis. She stayed there until she made a connection with a St. Louis and San Francisco Railroad car to Marionville, in southwest Missouri. She hired a wagon and driver to transport her forty miles through the steep, forested Ozarks to the home of Captain Powell."

Later, in her own book on caves, Ella described this journey:

> The drive of forty miles is delightful, but can be divided into two of twenty each by a stop at Galena. The road, for the most part, is naturally macadamized and is through a most charming country whose roughness and beauty increase as the journey advances. At first it advances along fertile valleys between wooded hills, crossing many times a shallow stream of water so clear as to afford no concealment for an occasional water moccasin.

In his book *Missouri Caves in History and Legend*, Dwight Weaver explains that the first "show cave" in Missouri was Mark Twain Cave, near Hannibal, opened in 1886. That year Truman Powell moved his family from Lamar, Missouri, in Barton County to Stone County and started a newspaper, *The Oracle*, in Galena. He learned about Marble Cave, which had been a successful guano mine in the 1880s, and began to write about it and other caves in Stone County. William Lynch, a Canadian, came to Stone County, bought Marble Cave, and opened it to visitors in 1894; it became the third show cave in Missouri. "Visitors entered by climbing down a long ladder into the gigantic, domed Cathedral Room, where a platform was built and a piano installed. William Lynch's young daughters . . . entertained visitors by playing the piano and singing opera tunes."

Truman S. Powell, Galena newspaper publisher, was instrumental in
opening Marble Cave to the public in 1886. He "provided kind and valuable assistance" to Luella, but she noted "his blessing on the breakfast
was lost in so fervent a prayer for the safe and successful accomplishment
of the undertaking, it seemed inconsiderate not to present the reassuring
appearance of inexhaustible endurance." (Courtesy of the State Historical
Society of Missouri)

Unfortunately the cave was too remote for visitors less intrepid than Ella Owen, and Lynch closed the cave and moved
away. During his decade-long absence, William Powell, one of
Truman Powell's sons, moved nearby and started showing the
cave without Lynch's "knowledge or consent." Lynch eventually returned, however, and Powell had to turn it over to him.

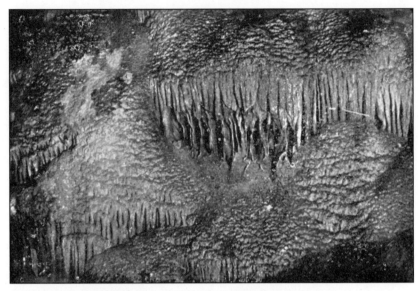

Blondy's Throne Room in Marble Cave. Luella wrote, "The guide begins at once to mention the difficulties of getting there. But if you insist upon it he will go." She reported that the formation was named for "a fair-haired, intrepid, and daring fifteen-year-old boy, named Charles Smallwood, who assisted a writer in exploring the cave in early 1883." Today the story is told that Charles Smallwood, exploring the cave alone, got lost and spent the night on the formation. When rescuers found him they named it "Blondy's Throne." The throne was so large it formed a wall in the adjoining room. Luella climbed the throne and estimated it was about one hundred feet high. (*Cave Regions of the Ozarks and Black Hills,* courtesy of the Western Historical Manuscript Collection, Columbia)

Another Powell son, Waldo, lived near a smaller but beautiful cave in Stone County that the Powells had first explored in 1896. In 1907 they bought "Fairy Cave," and opened it to the public.

Despite all her careful planning and her arduous efforts to arrive at a particular cave, Ella was not always successful in gaining access to it after she got there. Many cave owners were reluctant to guide her through a cave—in large part because she was a woman, but also because the caves were not developed for the comfort of tourists at the time as some were later. Entrance was usually gained by climbing down crude clay steps or rickety wooden ones, or even by being lowered into the cave with a rope and bucket. Once inside, only hand-held candles or flares were available to light the way—no flashlights, or electric lights, no two-way radios. Ella had to convince each doubting cave owner anew that she was a competent caver; sometimes she could not persuade them. Of one such encounter, she wrote humorously but ruefully:

> After some uneasy discussion about the means of entering the new cave, it was finally decided that the available rope was too short and not of sufficient strength. This was, of course, a disappointment but not a surprise, as a very peculiar quality in the rope used to enter caves of this kind had come to notice before. The peculiarity is, that a rope entirely above suspicion for the safety of a two hundred pound man, at once weakens and must be condemned when threatened with one hundred pounds of woman's weight.

Sometimes, though, Ella realized their fears were justified, so she made the best of her disappointment. This happened when she journeyed eagerly to Waldo Powell's Fairy Cave, now called Talking Rocks, which had previously been visited by only six people. To enter it, she and the guide would have to be lowered one hundred feet straight down in a large bucket. As Ella told it in her book:

> Each of the three men present kindly offered to go down and make the exploration with me, but that would have left only two at the windlass, and for a man's weight safety requires four. Should an accident occur, assistance would be necessary and some time lost in finding it; so to the undisguised satisfaction of one and the equally evident relief of the others, it was reluctantly decided that the trip must be given up, and therefore we are indebted to Captain Powell for the following description of Fairy Cave.

Swallowing her disappointment, she had to accept the secondhand description, which she included word for word in her book. Her gracious acceptance of concerns expressed for her safety no doubt relieved the owner as well as the personnel of other caves she visited.

Ironically, according to Dwight Weaver, Fairy Cave "was not the sole domain of men in the Powell family during their ownership." Truman Powell's granddaughter, Hazel Rowena Powell, later became a part of the Fairy Cave operation and in 1953 published a small guide to Missouri show caves, "the first book published that was devoted exclusively to Show Caves," according to Weaver. On their return to Marble Cave, the Lynch sisters went back to descending into the Cathedral Room to play the piano and eventually became managers of the cave, "becoming accomplished spelunkers and show cave operators." Genevieve wrote a poem about the Cathedral Room quoted in *Jewel of the Ozarks,* by Ronald L. Martin. It ends,

> Here, something lingers, subtle, fine
> Irradiations, veiled, divine
> God's temple and the age's tomb.

Ella, almost thirty years older than Genevieve Lynch, readily admitted that caves sometimes contained "a great many dangerous places," but she remained undaunted, even daring at times to explore without a guide. In writing about one such adventure, which took place in a cave near Thayer, Missouri, she told of drifting in a small boat down a "silently flowing river" while her young nephew, James Arthur Owen, and their guide—who had never floated that waterway—stayed behind and hung onto a coil of twine attached to the boat so they could pull it back. "The boat drifted along with surprising speed," she recalled, "so that the two scared faces peering after me were soon lost sight of."

In another cave, when the guide had to leave her alone with only one candle while he retraced his steps to recover forgotten equipment, she described the experience as "one of the great events of a lifetime. The entire absence of sound was indescribably awe-inspiring."

At a cave in the Black Hills of South Dakota, she and another nephew, Herbert Owen Jr., crawled through an opening too small for their guide and made their way over "extremely rough country" to the Niagara Room "to see a splendid waterfall formation." The guide later told her that she had been "where no lady had gone before." Actually, few men had gone there either.

Once while she was exploring Wind Cave in the Black Hills, Ella found herself confronted by a narrow passage with its floor sloping toward a two-foot wide abyss in the middle. She coped with the challenge, she wrote, "by placing a foot on either side of the open crevice; the first consideration, of course being safety and not grace."

Sometimes she risked jumping to reach her goal. Once, when a rope ladder reached only halfway down a wall and left her sitting on a ledge, her guide suggested she drop off and let him break her fall. She called this "rapid transit." Sometimes of course she simply fell by accident, reporting good-humoredly that "I have unexpectedly reached many coveted points in this simple manner."

Ella considered Marble Cave "the finest explored in Missouri." She had chosen to visit the cave in May, when the "strawberries were ripe and the weather without a fault." The entrance to the cave was "through a large sink-hole" with sloping sides. About half of the descent was achieved by scrambling down the broken rock, and the rest on a broad wooden stairway. Part of the exploration involved crawling through a seventy-foot passage, and in another part of the cave she climbed a "Spanish ladder made of a tall pine tree with stumps of branches to be used for hand holds, climbing over boulders."

When she decided that she had enough material for a book, including notes and photographs she had taken on her explorations, Ella set about writing. Her book reporting her own studies of caves focused on the caves in the Missouri Ozarks and the Black Hills of South Dakota, caves that had not been covered by Hovey. Dedicated to her mother, *Cave Regions of the Ozarks and Black Hills* was published in 1898. For fifty years it served as

Luella described the approach to Deadwood, South Dakota, by train on her second trip to the Black Hills with her small nephew Herbert Owen, Jr., as "twisting around the curves of the Hills clinging to the sides of the canyon." She reported that the "forests of pine and spruce look black in the distance and suggested the name of the Black Hills to the Indians who always have a reason for their names." The second trip was necessary because one cave owner had written her it would be "quite impossible" for him to send her a description of his cave for her book. (*Cave Regions of the Ozarks and Black Hills,* courtesy of the Western Historical Manuscript Collection, Columbia)

the only reference on Missouri caves, and it made her one of the region's best-known spelunkers/speleologists. A spelunker is one whose chief interest is in exploration, underground adventure, and esthetic appreciation. A speleologist has a geological background and is interested primarily in understanding the conditions that made caves. Luella Owen was both.

Following the example set in Hovey's book, she wrote her book for the lay reader, and its gentle humor and travelogue descriptions make it enjoyable reading even today, more than a century later. Informative, descriptive, and, at times even poetical when

Luella found the
"Chimes" forma-
tion in Crystal Cave
particularly beauti-
ful. (*Cave Regions of
the Ozarks and Black
Hills,* courtesy of the
Western Historical
Manuscript Collec-
tion, Columbia)

describing icy water flowing down glittering cave walls or blue calcite crystals, the book provides insights into the writer's wit, her values, and her depth of knowledge about her subject. Ella felt strongly about conservation of caves, writing that "the gift of beauty should always be honored and protected for the public good."

She opened the first chapter of her book with an excerpt from a poem by Thomas Moore:

> On mountains bright, with snow and light,
> We crystal hunters speed along,
> While grots and caves and icy waves,
> Each instant echo to our song;
> And when we meet with stores of gems
> We grudge not kings their diadems.

She then gave general information about caves, explaining that the largest and most important caves occur in limestone, and that the active agent in the process is, as she put it, "the comparatively gentle, invisible gas known as carbonic acid," which slowly eats away at the limestone. Missouri's limestone caves, she said, may be the most ancient in the world, and she added that even though the Ozarks were not as well known as some other cave areas, "the scenery is good, the climate delightful, and the caves worthy of visit." Although the book reads as if her cave explorations were done on one continuous tour, researchers believe that these field studies were actually conducted over a five- to seven-year period, probably beginning in 1892. Eventually, Ella's cave explorations began to wind down. During her caving experiences, she was able to contribute important proof, in 1896, that the Wind Cave of South Dakota was an extinct geyser, and the following year, that the Grand Canyon of the Yellowstone was the remains of a geyser basin. Her last scientific paper on caves, "Les Cavernes de Ha Ha Tonka," appeared in 1898.

During 1898, Ella began to concentrate again on studies of loess soil. In August 1897, in her flowing handwriting, she wrote Dr. Wright at Oberlin College, with whom she conducted an ongoing correspondence. She wanted to let him know of what she called "a recent find of great interest . . . a green, stone, grooved, and polished ax found in May 1897, imbedded in the loess, but not in a grave, near the top of the Missouri River bluff south of Atchison, Kansas." In a later letter, she wrote Wright,

> I thank you very cordially for your interest in the ax and shall try to show that it is not wasted. It was not possible for the ax to have been buried by wash from higher ground for the conclusive reason that there was no higher point than that where it lay buried at a depth of about four feet from the surface on top of the bluff two hundred and forty feet above the Missouri River low water mark.
>
> I have decided to take the ax and the affidavit to Detroit, where I shall arrive Tuesday, hoping the find may prove as interesting as I believe it to deserve.

In a paper titled "The Bluffs of the Missouri River," intended for her fellow geologists and focusing on the site of her childhood explorations, she wrote,

> The valley of the Missouri and a portion of that of the Mississippi are defined by bluffs of special geographical and geological interests. . . . These bluffs of Loess being well developed at the various cities along the Missouri, the deep cuts made through them for railroads, streets, and other purposes, offer exceptionally fine opportunities for the careful study of the still open question of its true origin and formation. Kansas City and St. Joseph are, perhaps, the best points for study. . . . The original undisturbed Loess of aqueous origin can be positively identified in many places about St. Joseph, by the numerous fresh-water shells imbedded and by pockets of sand.

Continuing her discussion of bluff formation, she cited the finding of the large stone ax imbedded in a bluff twenty miles south of St. Joseph, adding, "The ax came into the possession of the writer almost immediately after the discovery." It would be interesting to know the story behind that acquisition—and where it is today.

Near the end of the paper, she turned to a different topic of interest to her readers:

> Another noticeable feature of the Missouri River is the manner of the breaking up of the ice, which is entirely unlike that observed in some other important streams, such as the Hudson and Niagara. In these the first breaks occur along the banks and the ice begins to move out in a body; but in the Missouri the first cracks are across the channel, and are sometimes sufficiently straight and parallel to have the appearance of a wagon road. Later, cracks occur in all directions, and the water, flowing rapidly beneath, throws up spray that freezes into a heavy, frost-like rim around each cake which gives to the whole mass as it moves out, a peculiar, and often beautiful, appearance.

In 1900, Ella began to plan for what would be her most daring expedition, especially for her time and gender. She had already traveled extensively within the United States, and she now decided to make a year-long trip around the world as a working member of the American Geographic Society. She had been taken into this group at the same session as the famous explorer Admiral Robert E. Perry. Her friends always maintained she didn't even need a passport to travel because of her membership in so many worldwide geographical organizations. Her itinerary no longer exists, but biographers do know that it included the Philippines, China, and Germany, as well as many other countries.

By this time Ella was well known as a geologist. Although she shared duties at home with her sisters until their mother's death in 1911, her fame and her interest in loess had grown to the point that scholars traveled to St. Joseph to consult with her. When the controversial Lansing skeletons were found buried under loess in Lansing, Kansas, only twenty miles from St. Joseph, she served as both guide and hostess to visiting geologists.

Of the numerous geological papers Ella wrote, some were read at meetings of scientific associations, while others were published in academic journals. At the request of one of her mentors, George Frederick Wright, she wrote an article titled "More Concerning the Lansing Skeleton," which was included in the publication *Bibliotheca* in 1903. The Lansing skeleton, also known as the "fossil man of Kansas" and believed by many to be the oldest skeleton in this country, was found imbedded in loess on the Concannon farm at Lansing, Kansas. According to Ella, it continued "to maintain a firm hold on the attention of those distinguished for special work on the subjects involved in the determination of its early history." This article appeared as a companion piece to one written by Wright in which he had presented evidence to support the hypothesis that the loess of the Missouri and Mississippi Valleys was largely derived from sediment brought down by glacial floods, as opposed to the earlier belief that wind was primarily responsible for the distribution of the loess. In her article, Ella argued that geological evidence supported her contention of the existence of glacial man in the

Missouri valley. She summarized by saying, "On the banks of the Missouri, man was a witness to those great and rapid changes of terrestrial conditions connected with the closing stages of the glacial period; thus anew raising glacial geology to a most important rank among the historical sciences."

She read her paper, "The Loess at St. Joseph," at the meeting of the American Association for the Advancement of Science in January 1904; "Evidence of the Disposition of Loess" appeared in the *American Geologist* in 1905. Also in 1904, she traveled to St. Louis to present a paper at the American Association for the Advancement of Science, which had planned its meeting to coincide with the Louisiana Purchase Exposition. This was the first paper Ella had given in her home state.

In 1908 she presented a paper titled "The Missouri River and Its Future Importance to Europe" at the International Geographical Congress in Geneva. The paper was also published in the *Scottish Geographical Magazine*. On this trip she also went to Scotland to conduct genealogical research on the Cargill clan, ancestors of her mother's family, for a family history of the Owens and Cargills that she was planning to write.

At the beginning of the twentieth century, when age forty-seven was considered old—in fact, was the American life span—Luella Owen was at the height of her professional career. She had achieved her lifelong ambition of cave exploration and had written an informative and entertaining chronicle of her caving adventures. In addition, she was a geologist of international repute as well as a genealogist and talented portrait artist. An intrepid traveler, she traveled more extensively than anyone she knew and more than most women at the time.

In one of its tributes to this unique Missouri woman, the *St. Joseph News-Press* declared that she had taken as her philosophy the admonition to "Take the thing that lies nearest thee, shape from that thy work of art." Luella Agnes Owen did exactly that.

6

"Miss Juliette"

Ornithologist, Botanist, and Artist

If Juliette Amelia Owen had been born into almost any other family, her accomplishments would have been considered extraordinary, especially for the time in which she lived. As the youngest Owen daughter, however, she followed her older sisters Mary, who became a world-renowned folklorist, and adventurous Luella, who made a name for herself in a male-dominated scientific profession. Even so, "Miss Juliette," as she was known in St. Joseph, became a knowledgeable and nationally known ornithologist and botanist, though little is known about her work in these fields.

Petite, dark-haired, and fragile, Juliette was regarded as the beauty of the Owen family from her early childhood on. Not only more retiring by nature than her sisters, she was seemingly never as strong as they were and, as a result, was probably always more sheltered by her parents. She had problems with her eyes and often suffered from severe headaches. The *St. Joseph News-Press* described her as "unassuming and always interested in her callers rather than in herself." In another story, the *News-Press* declared that she "had a keen sense of humor and could regale her callers with stories of the early days of their families."

As a young woman, Juliette attended Dr. Martin's Female Academy. She then became a student at Patee Female Seminary (formerly Patee College) where she took courses in natural history, German, and painting. Although Mary and Ella liked to say they had always lived in the house on Ninth and Jules, the older children had moved from the Owen home on Sixth Street to the new house when it was completed in the late 1850s. Juliette had been the first of the children to be born in the new home James Owen built just before the Civil War, and she lived there all her life.

Although Juliette was more active socially than either Mary or Luella, she too (or her mother) made sure she spent the mornings at home studying. She chose such books as Thomas Nuttall's *A Manual of Ornithology in the United States* and the writings of Elliott Coues, the ornithologist and naturalist who helped found the American Ornithologists Union and later served as its president and editor of its publication. From 1876 to 1880, Coues was secretary and naturalist of the U.S. Geological and Geographic Survey of the territories, and he later edited the journals of Lewis and Clark and Zebulon Pike's account of his early explorations of the western rivers. He became well versed and interested in the history of the West.

Juliette was especially drawn, however, to the works of the artist John James Audubon, who had traveled up the Missouri River past her hometown in 1843. According to Authorine Phillips's *Arrow Rock*, Audubon, then almost sixty years old and famous for his paintings of American birds, traveled on the steamboat *Omega*, which was carrying supplies for trading posts owned by Pierre Chouteau Jr. He had a party of five assistants and hunters Chouteau had provided traveling with him. Although the *Omega* returned to St. Louis after delivering its supplies, Audubon and his party remained at Yellowstone until the fall of the year, reportedly having "made a very fine collection of animals" before their return. Juliette became a collector of Audubon books and information about the artist.

DE BUHDS.

Mary Alicia Owen's book *Old Rabbit the Voodoo and Other Sorcerers*, published in London in 1893, brings together a body of Juliette Owen's work that reveals her affection for the world around her. Juliette's lifelong interest in birds is reflected in this gathering of many of the birds she studied. (Courtesy of the State Historical Society of Missouri)

Like Mary and Ella, Juliette also read widely in periodicals dealing with her area of interest, natural history, especially the emerging field of ornithology, the study of birds. She enjoyed bird watching, and delighted in bringing the birds she observed to life in her watercolors. She became knowledgeable enough about birds to qualify for associate membership in the exclusive American Ornithologists' Union and to contribute sightings to its publication. One of only ten women who achieved this distinction, she was a member of the organization for nearly forty-six years. Contemporary articles about her always proudly listed the many organizations to which she belonged and seldom failed to report that she and her sister Luella were listed in *American Men of Science*. She was also a fellow of the American Association for the Advancement of Science, a member of the Washington Biological Society, the American Museum Society, the New York Academy of Sciences, the American Nature Society, the American Forestry Association, and the Washington Academy of Sciences. Like her sisters, Juliette also participated in such groups as the Daughters of the American Revolution and was an active member of Christ Episcopal Church.

In her study of the journal *Forest and Stream*, Juliette learned that the bird population was dwindling nationwide. The staff of *Forest and Stream* worked vigorously to promote an awareness of the need for laws to protect not only birds but other animals that were disappearing, and Juliette joined enthusiastically in this effort to preserve wildlife. According to *Who's Who in St. Joseph*, she wrote numerous pamphlets and several series on birds of America. She submitted her articles to the journal for publication under a pen name, presumably intending, like her sisters, to write under her own name once she had established herself. However, she discovered a British author whose name was J. A. Owen—Jean Allen Owen—who wrote on subjects similar to those Juliette wrote about and who even contributed to one of Juliette's favorite journals, *Forest and Stream*. So Juliette continued to write under her pen name, which she never publicly disclosed. Only one work has been found under her own name, *A Memorial to the*

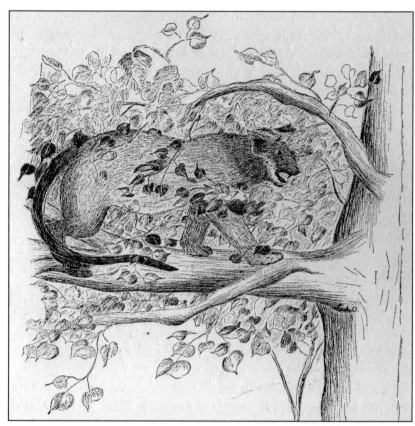

Juliette's drawing of "De Painteh" evokes the fearsome nature of the panther in the story Mary heard from "Aunt Em'ly." Taken in as a "kitten" to
be a pet, the panther soon revealed his true nature. (Courtesy of the State
Historical Society of Missouri)

Nations of the Air, in which she mourns the fact that "God created
birds . . . and it will be written that man who was made in His
image annihilated them." It ends saying, "When . . . at each awak-
ening spring they come to struggle for existence in the world's
arena for a time, it would seem their exultant paean could not be
in celebration of the life and love of earth, but as the salutation of
the gladiators of old to their ruler: 'Hail Imperator, those who are
about to die salute thee.'"

When the Missouri Audubon Society was formed in St. Louis, Juliette immediately became a life member of this first Audubon organization in her home state. She also became a member of the National Association of Audubon Societies. She worked with fellow society members to encourage legal protection of the native bird population, especially those that were rapidly dying out. Unfortunately it was too late for the passenger pigeons, which had already disappeared. Madeline Matson, in *Food in Missouri*, reports that the last passenger pigeon, "the most numerous bird ever to exist on earth," was killed in 1900. Juliette wrote articles for women's magazines advocating the protection of American wildlife, and she spent a great deal of her time reading about birds, observing them, and sketching and painting them in her delicate watercolors. She reportedly produced more than one hundred watercolor drawings of flowers and natural scenery about St. Joseph.

In 1914 Juliette was a founding member of the Humane Society of St. Joseph and Buchanan County and a member of the National Humane Society. She helped promote and advance national and international legislation for the conservation of wildlife and natural resources.

Numerous sources cite Juliette as the author of two books: *Ornithology and Botany in Northwest Missouri* and *Songs, Habits, and Protection of Birds*, but searches for these books have not proved successful. Certainly she worked on them for years but perhaps they were never published, or the unfinished manuscripts may have been destroyed when the Owen home was demolished several years after her death.

"Miss Juliette" was featured in numerous newspaper interviews and stories. One, published in the *St. Joseph News-Press* on October 25, 1943, tells that once a burglar, responding to her gracious ways, returned the loot he had stolen from her home. Miss Juliette relished telling the episode and said that after returning her property, he said, "I will come and see you again." She said she wanted to cry out, "Oh, no," but "felt it wouldn't be polite."

7

The Twilight Years

As Agnes Owen grew older and more frail, the three daughters living with her spent more time at home with their mother. She continued to manage the family estate with the help of Herbert and his son Stephen. When her brother John's children decided to sell their part of Burr Oak Grove, she kept her share to pass on to her children. In December 1911, Agnes Cargill Owen died at her home, with her five children and most of the grandchildren at her bedside. Only the two grandchildren who lived in Seattle could not be there. The minister from Christ Church, where she had been a member since its first service in 1851, conducted her funeral service in the Owen family parlor, and she was buried beside her husband and her two infant children. The death of this remarkable pioneer woman marked the end of an era in St. Joseph. Having managed the family fortune so well, she was one of the richest women of the city when she died, and her passing made each of her surviving children independently wealthy.

After their mother's death in 1911, the "literary sisters," as they were sometimes called, now had more freedom to travel, to entertain, or to work at their professions with fewer interruptions. But first, they had many decisions to make and duties to perform: writing letters and thank-you notes, disposing of their mother's personal possessions, and settling her estate. Like her

Agnes Cargill Owen was well regarded by the people of St. Joseph and by her children. Luella Owen expressed her devotion to her mother in her book *Cave Regions of the Ozarks and Black Hills,* published in 1898: "To My Mother This Book is affectionately dedicated." (Courtesy of the St. Joseph Historical Society)

husband before her, Agnes Owen left no will, and her property was divided equally among her five children. Agnes and James had taught their children the wisdom of keeping the family estate intact, and in turn they decided to keep the Owen family holdings together, with each heir continuing to draw a comfortable income.

After their mother's death, the sisters may have considered relocating from their childhood home. They no doubt received much unsought advice on this and other issues from family and friends. Mary might have enjoyed living in New York or even London, closer to her publishers and editors. For Ella, either New York or Washington, D.C., would have been nearer to the headquarters of her geographic and geological societies. Juliette, on the other hand, could hardly observe, paint, and write about Missouri birds and plants while living in the East. Missouri and the St. Joseph area provided resources for much of Mary's and Ella's work as well, and was home to them. Moreover, all three sisters drew on the companionship of one another and the company of their brother and his family. They also had to consider that they now ranged in age from fifty-two to sixty-one, late for single women to start life over in a new setting in the early twentieth century, and Mary may have remembered her homesickness during her year at Vassar. If they remained where they were, in the house that had long been paid for, their living expenses would be minimal to modest. Whatever their reasons, they ultimately decided to remain in St. Joseph, in the house in which they had grown up. In addition to their emotional ties to their native city, they had sound financial reasons for doing so.

They turned their attention to the duties at hand, reading and sorting old family papers and correspondence, learning more about their parents, grandparents, and more distant family members than they had previously known. Ella was especially interested in the genealogy of the Cargill and Owen ancestors and was writing a book on the subject, but Mary and Juliette must have found some details of their family history of interest as well, especially that of their father. All soon took up again the work to which they had devoted their energies for so many years.

In 1912, the year after Agnes Owen's death, Mary was scheduled to represent the United States at the International Folk-Lore Congress in London, and she was busy preparing the paper she would present. After reading her paper on "Rain Gods of the American Indians," in London, she traveled to Holland where

the paper was to be published as a book. She then took a "grand
tour" of Europe, which included a visit to Florence to visit the
grave of her friend, Charles Godfrey Leland, but she returned to
St. Joseph in good time to attend the wedding of her brother's
son, Stephen. As the years passed, the sisters continued to write,
work in their areas of interest, and attend conferences. Mary
employed a secretary to help the three of them keep up with
their correspondence and manuscripts. As she approached her
late sixties, she was still collecting folklore and writing poetry,
serving as president of the Missouri Folk-Lore Society, and was
both a leader and an active member of a literary/writers group
in St. Joseph that met monthly. She also traveled around the state
giving lectures on folklore at annual meetings of the Folk-Lore
Society and encouraging teachers and others to preserve the folk
traditions of Missouri.

Although she had carefully written down the songs she
learned from African American storytellers in St. Joseph and
published in *Voodoo Tales*, as well as the chants and songs given
to her by the Mesquakie she visited, Mary never showed much
interest in the English traditional songs Belden and his students
were working to collect, convinced all would soon be lost if not
preserved as soon as possible. In *Voodoo Tales*, she had mentioned
an English song her mother sang, "Poor Babes in the Woods,"
published in 1765 by Bishop Thomas Percy in *Reliques of Ancient
English Poetry* from a collection made a century earlier. The song
tells the story of the "poor little babes" who were "stolen away
one bright summer's day and lost in the woods." According to a
version Belden published:

> They sobbed and they sighed, and they bitterly cried
> Poor babes in the woods! They lay down and died.
> And when they were dead, the robins so red,
> Brought strawberry leaves and over them spread.

While others searched for songs originating in England or
what became known as "Child ballads" from *The English and
Scottish Popular Ballads* of "proven antiquity" published by James

Francis Child in the late nineteenth century, Mary promoted a more inclusive concept of "folk-lore" in its many manifestations. In an article published in *Missouri State Teachers Association Bulletin* in 1916 based on a talk she had given on "The Significance of Folk-Lore," she did not provide a special category for balladry or folk song but included it among "traditional narratives." She divided folklore into four categories: (1) superstitions, beliefs, and practices; (2) traditional customs; (3) traditional narratives; and (4) folk sayings.

She was obviously well aware of the effort going on to collect "all" of Missouri's traditional ballads, which Belden had first thought he and his students could do in a few years. And in her discussion of "The Significance of Folklore," Mary mentions ballads, but then adds, "The folk lyric, too, both secular and religious, belongs to folk-lore; likewise the rhymed recipe and bill of fare. (Why doesn't someone compile a folk cook book?)" She also included impromptu compositions that changed from singer to singer and recalled, "One 'hired hand's' song, called by the colored people 'Miss Kitty' and by white folk 'Solemn Sam' has new stanzas every time it is sung."

Mary's view of what a folklore society should do was much more comprehensive than that of most of the academic and student collectors, who founded state folklore societies primarily to search for Child ballads and other traditional English songs. Belden and others did eventually begin to include what they called "Native American Balladry" in their collections, but most of the books published during the first half of the twentieth century, including those of Belden and Vance Randolph, placed the Child ballads first when they published their collections.

Mary never sent Belden a copy of her mother's "Poor Babes in the Woods," perhaps realizing he had received copies from others. The one song she gave him was solidly based in Missouri history and folklore. It dealt with the death of Jesse James, who had been living on Lafayette Street in St. Joseph as Thomas Howard when Robert Ford shot him on April 4, 1882. She sent it in 1916, noting, "I heard it from a man who dug some post-holes for us. He said everybody used to sing it." Her version did not have the familiar refrain about Ford, "that dirty little coward that shot our Mr. Howard and laid poor Jesse in his grave," which became widely known. The song Mary contributed gives a down-to-earth account of the events of Jesse's early life, the wrongs his family suffered before and during the war, and his death, ending with a moral:

> And then one day, the papers say, Bob Ford got his
> rewarding:
> A cowboy drunk his heart did plunk. As you do,
> you'll git according.

During World War I, Mary, who was well known for her witty stories, was in great demand as a speaker at war bond rallies. On one such occasion, as she was returning home in a taxi, the driver commented as they passed a field, "That land belongs to three old maids. Why don't they plow it up and put it in potatoes to feed the starving people of Europe?"

Mary, not at all flustered, replied politely, "I will speak to my sisters about it when I get home," and did not mind repeating the story to amuse her friends.

Like the Civil War, World War I resulted in more opportunities for employment for women as well as opportunities to take on public roles as volunteers in war-related activities. The number of women in the workforce had gradually increased in the late nineteenth and early twentieth centuries, particularly in teaching, and during the war women began to fill jobs opening as men left for the service. In the fall of 1917, Luella Owen must have been amused to learn, as a newspaper reported, that twenty women and girls had replaced men in the shops of the Chicago, Burlington, and Quincy Railroad in St. Joseph, especially the report that "the women all wear overalls and jumpers."

Due to the effects of the war and the flu epidemic, the Missouri Folk-Lore Society became inactive after 1920. Belden had planned to publish his collection of ballads and folk songs along with

According to his widow, this is the last photograph made of Jesse James. Robert Ford killed James in his home in St. Joseph on April 3, 1882, as he stood on a chair to straighten a picture on the wall. Robert and Charles Ford were tried for the murder and found guilty but were pardoned by the governor. The song Mary Alicia quoted reported the fate of Robert Ford. (Courtesy of the State Historical Society of Missouri)

contributions from Mary as a volume of *Memoirs* of the American Folk-Lore Society. But, as he later reported in his autobiography: "I found that Miss Mary Owen of St. Joseph, president of our Missouri Society, on whom I had counted for part of the volume not devoted to ballads, was not interested in the scheme and was besides in poor health."

Whatever the state of her health in 1920, Mary Alicia Owen was ready to publish one more major work as the centennial of

Missouri statehood approached. In its centennial issue of October 1920, the *Missouri Historical Review* included her "Social Customs and Usages in Missouri during the Last Century" as its lead article. It is an affectionate, well-informed, and witty account of Missouri's famed frontier hospitality and social customs from the earliest European settlers to the first decades of the twentieth century, demonstrating her powers of observation and attention to detail. It describes picnics, church socials, parties, or "frolics," dances, holiday traditions, weddings, funerals, and many other events. Her accounts of weddings are gently satirical:

> [On the morning after the wedding, after breakfast] she and the bridegroom went to his people for the "infare." . . . There was an elaborate dinner, a still more elaborate supper, and dancing . . . the bridal festivities continued as long as either of the high contracting parties had a relative well enough off to give an entertainment, and wherever the bride went, the bridegroom, like Mary's little lamb, was sure to go.

The "virtual fever" of collecting folklore that had developed in the United States had focused primarily on songs brought by settlers of British origin. As historian Alan Havig notes, "A unique feature of Owen's narrative is the inclusion of French, Spanish, German, and Southern American contributions to the social life of late eighteenth and nineteenth century Missouri." "Social Customs and Usages in Missouri during the Last Century" has appeared in recent years in two anthologies. Folklorist W. K. McNeil reprinted it in 1984 in *The Charm Is Broken: Readings in Arkansas and Missouri Folklore,* noting that it was "must reading for anyone interested in the history and folklore of the Missouri frontier." In 2008 it was the lead article in *Filling Leisure Hours: Essays from the Missouri Historical Review 1906–2006.* Editor of the anthology Alan Havig noted that while recognizing "the early presence" of European immigrants in the state, the author "omits the 'customs and usages' of the state's non-whites." Perhaps Mary Alicia, who had become the first life member of the State Historical Society after it was founded in 1898, believed the members of the society were well informed about her earlier works on African American and Native American practices and her intention was to make more complete the story of Missouri settlers.

When the *Centennial History of Missouri,* compiled by Walter B. Stephens, appeared in 1921, the Owen family of St. Joseph was well represented. An entry on the family included detailed biographical information on James and Agnes Owen and their children, with paragraphs devoted to Mary Alicia, Luella, and Juliette. Both Mary and Luella had separate biographies of their own, and articles by both were included. Mary sent information about voodoo as it was practiced by King Alexander and other practitioners who visited St. Joseph to include in the section on Missouri Folklore in the *Centennial History.* Stephens wrote: "Miss Mary Owen of St. Joseph gathered information about voodooism in Missouri, showing this state to be a surprisingly rich field for that branch of folklore study. Gaining the confidence of the priests and priestesses of voodooism, this lady received from their own lips the story of . . . its rites and practices." The essay that developed from the information Mary provided is probably the most detailed account that has survived of what she learned about voodoo since, as she reported, she burned the book she had prepared on the subject.

The editor of the history commented on Mary's engaging personality that had won her so many friends: "With an acknowledged conversational gift, illuminated by flashes of a ready wit never known to carry a sting, her personality quickly impresses itself with a stamp that lingers well in the memory of a chance acquaintance and binds her old friends with ties both strong and pleasant."

An essay on "Missouri Underworld" in the centennial history quotes a paragraph on Greer Spring Canyon, north of Alton in Oregon County, written by Luella.

> Taking a last look at Greer spring with its cave river, grey walls, gay with foliage, and all the harmony of color and form combined in the narrow canyon that was once the body of a great cave, I recalled views on the Hudson River, and

in the mountains of Maryland, Virginia, and Pennsylvania, and others out in the Rocky Mountains in Colorado and the Wasatch in Utah, but among all these wonderful grandeurs and famous beauty, could remember no spot superior to this master-piece of the Ozarks.

Like Mary, Ella Owen also continued writing and attending conferences and presenting scientific papers as she grew older. In 1924, she presented a paper to the American Association for the Advancement of Science, which her mentor G. F. Wright had written before he died. In that same year, she donated an oil portrait she had painted of Dr. H. L. Fairchild to the association. In 1925, when she was seventy-three years old, she read a paper titled "Later Studies on Loess," to this organization when it met in Kansas City. The paper was a companion to an earlier article she had written, "Evidence of the Disposition of Loess."

Although this trip was only forty miles from home, it was tiring for Ella, and it proved to be the last time she left St. Joseph; age was beginning to catch up with her. But she still worked at home on the Owen and Cargill genealogies she was writing for her family history, including in it interesting and humorous family anecdotes not usually found in genealogies. In the last fifteen years of her life, Ella compiled comprehensive histories of the Owen and Cargill families, as well as shorter studies on a few more distant relatives—all in her beautiful, flowing handwriting.

Following the death of a favorite grandniece in 1924, all three sisters began to spend more and more of their time at home. Mary, however, had one last major contribution she wanted to make to her home state. After the new state capitol in Jefferson City was completed in 1917, state officials began to develop a museum on the spacious first floor of the building. Mary Alicia decided to provide a duplicate of the collection of Mesquakie artifacts she had donated to the Folk-Lore Society in England two decades earlier for the Missouri State Museum, which she finally managed a few years before her death. An article, "Indian Collection in the State Museum," by Mabel D. Thompson, published

Luella included this photograph of "Wilderness Pinery" in Oregon County in *Cave Regions of the Ozarks and Black Hills*. She mentions three caves she visited in Oregon County and wrote eloquently of Green Springs for *The Centennial History of Missouri*. (Courtesy of the Western Historical Manuscript Collection, Columbia)

in the *Missouri Magazine* of September 1931 includes illustrations of a large display of beadwork, ceremonial objects, and photographs. "These are duplicates of Indian beadwork sent by me to the English Folklore Society and at present in the University of Cambridge Museum of Archaeology and Ethnology," Mary wrote. "I would like to feel that my precious ornaments were safely housed. They can never be duplicated as they belong to a past even the red men are forgetting." Although, as Alison Brown points out, she knew that her "ornaments" were ceremonial objects for the Mesquakie, she, like others of the period, believed that collecting and preserving them to document a past in danger of disappearing was a duty not to be avoided.

When Mary Alicia donated the collection of Mesquakie artifacts to the Missouri State Museum shortly before her death, she included what she believed to be Black Hawk's Cup, which she said the daughter of the Sac warrior had given her. In the *Life of Black Hawk,* the Sac leader said, "I was born in the Sac Village on the Rock River in 1767." In the early 1830s, he led an uprising that became known as "Black Hawk's War." (Courtesy of the State Historical Society of Missouri)

Juliette had taught herself enough veterinary medicine to enable her to care for her pets and the many sick animals she had collected, and, according to a history of northwest Missouri, she translated German poetry into "graceful English." Her vision had deteriorated so much that she now had to curtail her reading, but she ran the household and often gave interviews about

Luella Owen wrote the first book on caves in Missouri and continued her work in geology and family history after completing her book. (Courtesy of the State Historical Society of Missouri)

the family after her older sisters became more reclusive during their last years.

Mary, who had become more plump with age, reportedly stopped trying to watch her weight. Often one or more of the three spent the entire day in bed; if they did get up, they sometimes didn't bother to get dressed. They wore wigs to cover their thinning hair, so they didn't have to worry about appointments with a hairdresser. Having conformed to social expectations all of their lives, they may have decided they were entitled to their eccentricities in old age. The sisters were well liked in their hometown, viewed fondly as somewhat eccentric but witty. Relatives often told stories of their eccentricities as they aged. Her sister Florence's great-grandson recalls a story told by his father Wallace, who took his fiancée to meet the elderly sisters. The bride-to-be was very allergic to cats, and the Owen house was full of "dozens, if not hundreds, of cats." The young woman sat through an hour or an hour and a half of her "interview," sniffling, sneezing, and wheezing. Ever afterward, the sisters lamented that "poor Wallace" had married such a frail and sickly woman.

After an active lifetime of scientific study, cave exploration, and world travel, Ella was the first of the three sisters to die. In early 1932, she began to weaken and, after developing pneumonia, she died peacefully in her bed on May 31, with all her siblings around her. After the services were read in the parlor, her casket was placed in the family mausoleum at Mount Mora. Her obituary declared,

> She [Luella] was an indefatigable student and was versed in astronomy and chemistry. As was the fashion in education in her youth, she was taught artistic accomplishments. Her talent for painting was quite marked, and her family has many fine specimens of her work with the brush, especially portraits. In her explorations of caves, she was fearless, though her daring caused many apprehensions to those closest to her.

After Ella died, Mary, who was eighty-two and always a realist, began to consider her own mortality. In 1934, after having premonitions of her death, she set to work preparing for her funeral, making a list of persons to be notified of her death and naming her pallbearers. Then, having completed these necessary practical matters, she resumed her normal routine. On the morning of January 5, 1935, she died in her sleep, just short of her eighty-fifth birthday. A local newspaper described the day:

"All yesterday afternoon and until late last night there was a constant stream of visitors at the house. Limousines rolled up to the front door where men and women prominent in the city life called to pay their respects."

In an excerpt from "Reminiscences of the Late Mary Alicia Owen," written for the *Kansas City Star* and reprinted in the *Missouri Historical Review* (92: 256–57), Robert M. Snyder wrote, "In her death, literature has lost a shining light." He described a visit he had made to St. Joseph to call on Mary Alicia. She was confined to her bed, but she sent word by her sister that she had an interesting episode in early Missouri history that she was willing for someone to use. Without permitting him to enter her bedroom, she told him the following story while he listened from an adjoining room:

> In the early days of St. Joseph history bands of Indians frequently would come to the settlement to trade with Joseph Robidoux, founder of the town. One of these bands brought with them a young white girl captive, with whom a son of Robidoux promptly became enamored. The young man decided to possess her at any cost. The matter however was arranged with no great difficulty. The elder Robidoux had on hand a quantity of apples of which the Indians seemed particularly fond and a bargain was soon struck whereby the captive was relinquished for a few bushels of apples. Young Robidoux took possession of his property and thereafter the girl was known as Apple Mary.

After the death of Luella and Mary, Juliette kept busy. About a year before her death, she began to dispose of the various collections of her sisters as well as curios, manuscripts, and books. She continued to live in the family home with the spacious grounds where she sheltered and cared for pigeons, cats, and other stray animals. About a year before her death, with the United States in World War II, Juliette wrote whimsically, "I am not doing any other war work. I did contribute something to Britches for Britain, but britches begin at home and there is always someone needing a pair."

Juliette became the keeper of the Owen family legacy after her sisters died. She gave many interviews about the achievements of her family. (Courtesy of the State Historical Society of Missouri)

On October 25, 1943, after having been ill for several months with "heart weakness," Juliette died in the room in which she had been born almost eighty-four years earlier. She had outlived all her siblings; Herbert had died in the summer of 1936 and Florence in 1940. Juliette left behind a niece and four nephews. Her birthday celebration, which had been planned for November 3, was never held. Instead, the week before her birthday,

The Owen family mausoleum is near the front gateway in St. Joseph's historical Mount Mora Cemetery. (Photograph by Christopher Schroeder)

following services in Christ Episcopal Church chapel, she was interred in the family mausoleum at Mount Mora Cemetery. Family members had to find homes for the thirty-seven cats and other creatures she was caring for.

A *St. Joseph News-Press* article on October 29, 1943, said of Juliette: "She never knew but one home . . . but her outlook was as broad as the wide world, and her love for her fellow beings extended to all who came to her in their need."

After living their adventurous and productive lives, the three famous Owen sisters had finally crossed that invisible bridge, according to legend known to the ancient native tribes as "the road to Paradise." Perhaps all shared the sentiments about death expressed in a poem written by Mary in her later years.

> FINIS
> What heaven will be, I cannot guess
> I may like or may not,
> If I could choose I never would
> Go far from this dear spot.
> But choice is not for mortals
> So, brokenly, I cry,
> O beautiful world, good-bye, good-bye,
> O beautiful world, good-bye.

8

The Legacy of the Owen Sisters

Even viewed from the vantage point of the twenty-first century, the accomplishments of Mary Alicia, Luella, and Juliette Owen inspire notice, admiration, and respect. But in order to understand and appreciate the achievements and contributions of this unique trio of women, one needs to take a step back in time to recall the era that produced them.

The Owen sisters lived through tumultuous times from pioneer days in western Missouri through the first decades of the twentieth century. Mary and Luella were old enough to remember the Civil War. As children and grandchildren of Southern sympathizers, they experienced the tensions resulting from life in a bitterly divided state before, during, and after the war. In the last decades of the nineteenth century and early twentieth century, the three sisters saw St. Joseph grow from a frontier village with muddy, unpaved streets into a modern city with telephones, electric lights, and automobiles to replace horse-drawn carriages. Born in the early years of the woman's liberation movement, they were contemporaries of such women as Susan B. Anthony, Harriet Beecher Stowe, and Lucretia Mott, leaders in the struggle for woman's rights. They lived long enough to see the historic Nineteenth Amendment to the U.S. Constitution grant women the right to vote. Unfortunately, the Buchanan county clerk's office does not have registration records for the 1920s, and we do not know if they took advantage of that right.

The Civil War had hastened the emancipation of women, both by creating more opportunities for employment and by creating a greater need for workers. According to Mary Elizabeth Massey in *Women in the Civil War,* "The war acted as a springboard from which women leaped into spheres formerly reserved only for men." Nevertheless social restrictions for middle-class women remained. The Owen women were fortunate to grow up in a family that valued education for girls as well as boys during a time when education for females was neither highly valued nor widely available. It was an era when middle-class women were expected to marry young and spend their lives as ornamental companions and hostesses for their husbands while at the same time serving as homemakers and rearing and educating their children. Nevertheless, Agnes and James Owen supported their daughters' formal schooling, allowed them to pursue their individual interests, and provided the means for them to do so. They taught their daughters how to manage money and to keep financial records. Some biographers believe they encouraged or at least welcomed the decisions of Mary, Luella, and Juliette to remain single, foreseeing potential pitfalls in marriage. Each of the sisters developed her own special interest early in life and became skillful in juggling the normal social activities expected, while at the same time devoting herself to a satisfying career. At times, this process entailed activities not wholly approved of by their parents, but apparently each of them used the necessary strategies to cope with disapproval in carrying out their work.

Mary studied astronomy, ethnology, and archaeology, but she will be best remembered for her contributions to the preservation of Missouri's folk heritage and for her efforts to record the cultural traditions of the many ethnic groups in the St. Joseph area. As Mary Allcorn wrote, Mary Alicia Owen's books, short stories, and articles provide a wealth of information about voodoo magic and black and Indian lore in Missouri. Allison Brown, a British anthropologist, believes that Mary's anecdotal notes in letters and comments to her friends and family help us see the American Indians as real people rather than simply nameless objects for study and provide valuable insights into what was a remarkable cross-cultural relationship.

Some scholars, while recognizing the value of the artifacts she preserved and the information she provided relating to her collection, have questioned some of her findings, her methods of collecting, and her attitudes toward Native American culture. Brown, who has studied the Owen collection of Mesquakie artifacts in Cambridge, wrote that Mary "clearly understood the significance of many of the objects to the Tribe and appreciated that selling them was often a last resort. . . . Given that she recognized the symbolic value of so many of the objects, it is initially very disturbing that she removed so many." She later comments that Mary "considered her research to be almost a duty," believing that if she did not acquire the artifacts they would be lost forever. Brown considers *Folk-lore of the Musquakie Indians of Missouri* "undoubtedly one of the most important documents concerning the Mesquakie to emerge from the nineteenth century. Although Owen's writing style is somewhat lacking in today's language of anthropological objectivity, it conforms to the standards of ethnographic monographs of her day and displays a noticeable compassion." Brown also notes that Mary Owen did not "cross boundaries established by her subjects," and Greg Olson wrote that while "she initiated exchange of stories, they controlled . . . what they were willing to reveal."

Olson, who has worked closely with Ioway and Sac and Fox historians, points out, however, that tribal historians have found she made some factual errors and misinterpreted some of the information shared with her. It appears that *"Folk-Lore of the Mesquakie contained as much romance and poetry as it did scientific fact,"* he wrote, adding that her idealization of characters in fiction she wrote at the time also marked some of her scholarly work. He noted, "She lived and worked at a time when popular American culture harbored a generally idealized and nostalgic view of Native peoples." The view of the time, expressed in both art and literature, was that the stereotypical "noble savage" represented a culture doomed to vanish as European "civilization" advanced westward. Contemporary American Indian historians have found that Mary misinterpreted some of the information she gathered, and one of the most troublesome aspects of her work is her use of terms to identify members of the tribe and their beliefs. Although these identifiers such as "brave," "squaw," and "savage" were in common use at the time, scholars now realize they reflect the "racially condescending" attitudes that prevailed earlier.

Similar observations could apply to some of her work relating to African American residents of the St. Joseph area. Her affection for her "aunties" sometimes appears patronizing, but *Voodoo Tales* is still considered a valuable contribution to the oral literature of the time, and a reprint of the book appeared in 1999. Although she destroyed her manuscript on voodoo, she did provide detailed information relating to the practice for the *Centennial History of Missouri,* so some of the information she collected about voodoo was preserved.

Always interested in "humanity in all its manifestations," Mary belonged to many organizations and was a hardworking and dedicated participant in many local efforts to preserve Missouri's history. When Belden finally published *Ballads and Folksongs Collected by the Missouri Folk-Lore Society* in 1940, it was dedicated to her memory. He listed some of her many honors: "Honorary Member of the British Folk-Lore Society, Councillor and Life Member of the American Folk-Lore Society, President of the Missouri Folk-Lore Society 1908–1935."

In each of the many organizations to which she belonged, she was a valued and involved leader. A memorial in the *Missouri Historical Review* described her achievements and expressed the admiration many felt for her:

> International authority of Indian tribal customs, student of folklore, author of repute at home and abroad, brilliant conversationalist, and first life member of the State Historical Society of Missouri, Miss Mary Alicia Owen held a high place in our culture. Modesty and independence were united with

mind and industry. Patience and poise characterized work and attitude. Retiring, somewhat mystical yet stimulatingly ironical at times, and always charged with anecdote and tale, her conversation was a precious memory to privileged friends. She was endowed with unusual force and power, possessed one of the most penetrating minds I have ever met and a personality so lovable that it charmed all who came within its influence. These will live long in memory and her scholarly works will endure.

Luella Owen's book, *Cave Regions of the Ozarks and the Black Hills,* for more than fifty years the only reference on Missouri caves, continues to make interesting reading today with its anecdotes and descriptions of the features of caves she visited in Missouri and in the Black Hills. A reprint of her "classic book" appeared in 1970, and Dwight Weaver notes it was "the first book to focus attention on the geology of Missouri caves." She mentions Marble Cave, Fairy Cave, Gentry Cave, Sugar Tree Hollow Cave, Pine Run Cave, Hermit Cave, Wolf's Den Cave, and Reynard Cave in Stone County, and Greer Spring, Bat Cave, and Grand Gulf in Oregon County. In *Missouri Caves in History and Legend,* Weaver wrote, "she noticed the destruction" that was occurring in caves and "spoke out against it." He quotes her plea:

Unfortunately most of the caves in this region [the Ozarks] have been deprived of great quantities of their beautiful adornment by visitors who are allowed to choose the best and remove it in such quantities as may suit their convenience and pleasure. Those who own the caves, and those who visit them, would do well to remember that if all the natural adornment should be allowed to remain in its original position it would afford pleasure to many persons for an indefinite time; but if it is removed, broken, and scattered, the pleasure of a few will be comparatively little and that short-lived. The gift of beauty should always be honored and protected for the common good.

Although, as Weaver notes, "hers was a voice crying in the wilderness" at the time, later cave historians including Weaver still work to ensure the preservation of the natural beauty of Missouri's caves.

Luella was also a knowledgeable observer of the Missouri River and wrote often of it. She was a pioneer for women interested in geology, a field that had not previously welcomed women. The acceptance by fellow geologists of this unique "nonprofessional" scholar opened the door at least a crack to women who came after her. She was a talented portrait painter and contributed many important items to the ancestral history of the family through her interest in genealogy and history.

Although Juliette was less in the public eye than were Mary and Luella, she too left her mark on the world in a number of ways. She gained admission to professional scientific organizations previously closed to women. She was quietly but actively engaged in advocating the protection of birds and other wildlife. She was a gifted water color artist, and although the whereabouts of few of her paintings are known today, she contributed evocative drawings to Mary's first book. When the Owen house on Ninth and Jules was demolished in 1949, the newspaper reported that observers could see that "books and papers and a broken bust of Schiller lay on the floor." Perhaps it was the poems of the German poet Schiller that Juliette had translated into "charming and graceful English."

Mary Alicia, Luella, and Juliette Owen did indeed dare to be different from their female contemporaries, and in the doing, made their impact felt. The writings of the remarkable Owen sisters are still read in scientific, historical, and art circles more than half a century after their deaths.

Epilogue

In 1848, just two years before Mary Alicia Owen was born, the Seneca Falls Convention of 1848 initiated a lengthy conflict that even today has not yet been totally resolved, but which began to change the way Americans viewed and treated women. No woman's rights movement had existed in this country before that time. The Seneca Falls Convention produced a groundbreaking document known as the Declaration of Rights and Sentiments that borrowed unashamedly from the Declaration of Independence, opening with the words, "When in the course of human events . . ." and continuing, "We hold these truths to be self-evident: that all men and women are created equal; that they are endowed by their Creator with certain inalienable rights; that among these are life, liberty, and the pursuit of happiness; that to secure these rights governments are instituted, deriving their just powers from the consent of the governed." The document went on to list eighteen injustices women endured followed by a set of resolutions to address these wrongs.

Four determined women led the woman's rights movement in the United States. Two of them, Lucretia Coffin Mott and Elizabeth Stanton, were the principal organizers of the Seneca Falls Convention, and Stanton was the primary author of the Declaration of Rights and Sentiments. The other two key national figures of the woman's rights movement were Lucy Stone and Susan B. Anthony. In their quest to achieve equal rights for women, these women and their supporters not only worked to change or eliminate laws that oppressed women, they also tried to change the male-dominated society's perception of women as being inferior to men, and they worked with equal zeal to persuade women to believe in themselves and claim for themselves all the benefits of citizenship.

By the last two decades of the nineteenth century, under the leadership of these four women and their fellow activists, new fields of employment were opening to women, such as office work and retail sales. A few middle- and upper-class women, including the Owen sisters, were already pursuing careers in a variety of professions. Prior to the Civil War, writing had been one of the few occupations open to women, although many had been denied the right to publish what they wrote. Now many more wrote—mostly in diaries and journals, but also in magazines, newspapers, and even books—among whom Mary Alicia and Luella Owen led the way in Missouri.

Another Missourian, Emily Newell Blair from Joplin, worked tirelessly for change, focusing her efforts on the suffrage issue— helping to win the right for women to vote. Before that victory was achieved, women had to achieve their political goals by enlisting the help (votes) of their husbands and other like-minded men. Blair also made her voice heard through her writing for numerous magazines, such as *Cosmopolitan* and *Century.* In addition, she was the editor of *The Missouri Woman,* which carried articles on woman's rights and the progress toward suffrage.

In their book *Into the Spotlight: Four Missouri Women,* Margot Ford McMillen and Heather Roberson write that in 1916, when the National Democratic Convention was held in St. Louis, suffragists demonstrated for a suffragist plank in the party platform by forming a ten-block-long "Golden Lane." Each woman carried a yellow parasol and wore a yellow sash inscribed with the words "Votes for Women." They stood in a silent line on Locust Street where male delegates leaving the convention hall had to walk past them. The women's strategy worked. The delegates grudgingly added "Votes for Women" to their platform for the presidential election.

On April 5, 1919, Missouri governor Frederick D. Gardner signed a law allowing women to vote in the presidential election.

Not long after the law was signed, Blair wrote the foreword for an issue of the *Missouri Historical Review* that focused on the suffrage movement. A few months later, the United States Congress passed the historic Nineteenth Amendment, declaring that the right to vote "shall not be denied . . . on account of sex." Finally, the amendment was ratified on August 26, 1920.

The many changes in the status of women in the United States have not come easily or spontaneously; women have worked untiringly for more than 150 years to bring about the degree of equality they enjoy today, although the goal has not been completely accomplished on such issues as open access to all jobs for which they are qualified and equal pay for equal work.

For Further Reading and Research

The American Woman: Who Was She? edited by Anne Firor Scott (Englewood Cliffs, N.J.: Prentice Hall, 1971), is a relatively brief (182 pages) review of the changing role of women in American society in the century following the Civil War—the period in which the Owen sisters lived. This book includes excerpts from leading theoreticians of feminism, such as Elizabeth Cady Stanton, Charlotte Perkins Gilmore, and Carrie Chapman Catt, as well as a copy of the document "Declaration of Sentiments," which was adopted at the historic Woman's Rights Convention in Seneca Falls, New York, and is often credited with being the opening salvo in the battle for woman's rights.

Cave Regions of the Ozarks and Black Hills, by Luella Agnes Owen (Cincinnati: Editor Publishing, 1898), offers a very readable description of Luella Owen's cave explorations and provides interesting insights into the author's knowledge and personality.

Charles Godfrey Leland: A Biography in Two Volumes, by Elizabeth Robin Pennell (Boston: Houghton Mifflin, 1906) is a useful resource for more information about Mary Alicia Owen's lifelong friend and mentor.

"Ever Toward the Setting Sun They Push Us: American Indian Identity in the Writings of Mary Alicia Owen," by Greg Olson (master's thesis, University of Missouri, Columbia, 2009), is an interesting and well-researched resource.

The Half Not Told: The Civil War in a Frontier Town, by Preston Filbert (Mechanicsburg, Penn.: Stackpole Books, 2001), presents a grim overview of life in St. Joseph during the Civil War—the divided loyalties of its citizens, the often harsh Union occupation, and the devastation wrought by guerrillas.

Hardship and Hope: Missouri Women Writing about Their Lives, 1820–1920, edited by Carla Waal and Barbara Oliver Korner (Columbia: University of Missouri Press, 1997), is an anthology that covers approximately a century, starting before Missouri became a state and stopping the year that the Nineteenth Amendment to the U.S. Constitution was ratified, giving women the vote. Among the authors are Kate Chopin, Carry Nation, and Laura Ingalls Wilder. Many of the selections are letters or diaries.

The Incredible Owen Girls, by Jean Fahey Eberle (St. Louis: Boar's Head Press, 1977), is a must-read for anyone interested in a closer look at the daily lives of Mary, Luella, and Juliette. This book is out of print but paperback copies are still available at online sources such as *Amazon.com.*

History of the Growth and Development of Saint Joseph, by Nellie Utz (mimeographed copies in the St. Joseph Public Library and the St. Louis Public Library), provides a brief but fascinating history of the short-lived Pony Express.

Missouri Caves in History and Legend, by H. Dwight Weaver (Columbia: University of Missouri Press, 2008) examines the historical and cultural significance of Missouri caves from prehistoric times to the twenty-first century, discussing early cave exploration and research, including that of Luella Owen.

Seneca Falls and the Origins of the Woman's Rights Movement, by Sally G. McMillen (New York: Oxford University Press, 2008), is a timely book that serves to remind readers of the struggles of women of the late 1800s and early 1900s who campaigned so vigorously for women's rights. The author describes the lives and contributions of Susan B. Anthony and Lucy Stone, among others.

The Southern Lady: From Pedestal to Politics 1830–1890, by Anne Firor Scott (Chicago: University of Chicago Press, 1970) is included here because, given St. Joseph's Southern heritage and the fact that the Owen sisters' parents had themselves emigrated from the South, it is a good source to help the reader better understand the stance of James and Agnes Owen as well as that of Mary, Luella, and Juliette regarding women's rights.

In addition to these sources, the reader is urged to consider reading works by Mary Alicia and Luella Owen. Mary's short stories, such as "The Taming of Tarias," can be found on the Internet, and many of her articles and books are readily available in various public libraries, the Missouri History Museum in St. Louis, and the State Historical Society of Missouri in Columbia. The Missouri Folklore Society papers are at the University of Missouri Western Historical Manuscript Collection in Columbia; Mary's collection of Mesquakie artifacts and correspondence relating to the collection are at the Missouri State Museum in Jefferson City; and clippings relating to the family and copies of many of Mary's publications are in the St. Joseph Public Library main branch at 927 Felix Street. Luella's delightful book, *Cave Regions of the Ozarks and Black Hills,* may be found on the Internet and read onscreen or downloaded without charge.

Iron-Jawed Angels, a documentary film available on DVD, is another resource that dramatically presents the story of two woman's rights activists—Alice Paul and Lucy Burns—who risked their lives in their effort to help American women win the right to vote.

Index

About the Author

Doris Land Mueller teaches at St. Louis Community College and is the author of *M. Jeff Thompson: Missouri's Swamp Fox of the Confederacy* (University of Missouri Press), as well as five children's books, including *Small One's Adventure*, *The Best Nest*, and *Marryin' Sam*. She lives in Valley Park, Missouri.